The Characters of Christmas

Joshua Rhoades

Published by Joshua Paul Rhoades, 2024.

THE CHARACTERS OF CHRISTMAS

First edition. December 19, 2024.

ISBN: 979-8227593153

Written by Joshua Rhoades.

Also by Joshua Rhoades

Courage Under Fire: David's Stand On The Battlefield
Jonah's Journey: Voices Of Redemption And Lessons In Obedience
The Furnace Of Faith: 12 Principles From The Heat Of Faith
Whispers of Hope: Inspiring Stories of Men's Prayers In Scripture
Frontier Legends: The Oregon Dream
Elijah: A Beacon Of Boldness
HOOK, LINE & SAVIOUR - Faith Reflections from Fishing
Driven By Faith: Motor Racing Inspired Christian Life
30 Day Devotional - Bold and Strong- Coffee Devotions for a Courageous Christian Walk
Authentic Christianity: The Heart of Old Time Religion
Consider The Ant - God's Tiny Preachers
Flee Fornication: The Plea For Purity
Renewed Hope- How to Find Encouragement in God
Sounding The Call - The Voice of Conviction
The Altar - Where Heaven Meets Earth
The Bible's Battlefields- Timeless Lessons from Ancient Wars
The Sacred Art of Silence - How Silence Speaks in Scripture
Under Fire- The Sanctity of the Traditional Biblical Home
Who Is on the Lord's Side? A Call to Righteousness
What Is Truth? - From Skepticism to Submission
First and Goal- Faith and Football Fundamentals
From Dugout to Devotion- Spiritual Lessons from Baseball
Par for the Course- Faith and Fairways
The Believer's Pace- Tools for Running Life's Marathon
The Immutable Fortress- Security in God's Unchanging Nature
Biblical Bravery
Deer Stands and Devotions: A Hunter's Walk with God

Jesus Knows- Our Hearts, Our Responsibility
Restoration - Setting The Bone
Spiritual 911- God's Word for Life's Emergency's
The Freedom of Forgiveness
The Jezebel Effect - Ancient Manipulations Modern Lessons
The Shout That Stopped The Saviour
The Time Machine Chronicles: Old Testament Characters
Anchored In Truth Exploring The Depths of Psalm 119
Biblical Counsel on Anger
Proverbs' Portraits The Men God Mentions
Stumbling in the Dark - The Dangers of Alcohol
Guarding the Wicket Protecting Your Faith and Game
The Champion's Faith - Wrestling and Achieving Spiritual Victory
Scriptural Commands for Modern Times Living God's Word Today Volume 1
Scriptural Commands for Modern Times Living God's Word Today Volume 2
Scriptural Commands for Modern Times Living God's Word TodayVolume3
The Greatest Gift
A Christmas Journey of Faith
Daughter Of The King: Embracing Your Identity In Christ
Determination and Dedication Building Strong Faith As A Young Man
Walking Through Walls God's Power to Part the Storms of Life
David's Song Of Deliverance Praising God Through Every Storm
From Weakness to Warrior: Gideon's Transformation
Why Did Jesus Weep?
Living For God The Call To Be A Living Sacrifice
My Mind Is In A Fog What Do I Do?
Turning The Page Written By Grace
The Calling and Greatness of John the Baptist
For Such a Time Esther's Courageous Stand
From Brokenness To Beauty Written By The Pen of Grace
The Ultimate Guide to Massive Action- From Plans to Reality
A Heart Of Conviction
Serving In The Shadows
Repentance Revealed The Road Back To God
The Chief Sinner Meets The Chief Saviour Reflections On I Timothy 1:15

Answer The Call - 31 Days of Biblical Action
The Birthmark of the Believer
Reflections on Calvary's Cross
The Kingdom Builder Paul's Bold Proclamation of Christ
The Animal Of Pride
The Reach That Restores Christ Love For The Broken
Paul- The Many Roles of a Servant of Christ
Unshakeable Faith- 31 Days of Peace in God's Word
O Come, Let Us Adore Him- A Christmas Devotional
The Shepherd's Voice
The Trail From Vision To Mission
Enabled- Living God's Purpose With Power
Held Back But Not Defeated
The Enoch Walk
The Power and Precision of God's Word
The Children Who Found Christmas
Hearts of Valor - Faithful in the Call
Why It Matters Finding Hope in Moments of Frustration
The Wild West Lives On McCall Family Adventures
Igniting Courage Fueling Your Heart To Serve The Lord
The Characters of Christmas

Dedication

To you, dear reader,

This book is for those who seek the heart of Christmas and desire to know the One at its center: Jesus Christ. It is a celebration of the greatest story ever told—not just a story of angels, shepherds, and wise men, but the story of the Savior who came to redeem a broken world.

From the moment of His miraculous birth in Bethlehem, Jesus' life became the hinge on which all of history turns. He is the thread that weaves together the characters of Christmas—the One who called Mary to trust, Joseph to obey, shepherds to rejoice, and wise men to seek. Every person in this story finds their purpose, their joy, and their redemption in Him, and so do we.

To those who long to know the Savior more deeply, this book is for you. Let Mary's faith point you to the One who keeps His promises, even when they seem impossible. Her surrender to God's plan reflects the heart of the Savior who surrendered heaven's throne to come to earth for us.

To those who feel the weight of life's uncertainties, this book is for you. Joseph's quiet obedience points to Jesus' own faithfulness to the Father's plan, even when it led Him to the cross. His strength and resolve mirror the Savior's unwavering determination to fulfill His purpose of redemption.

To those searching for peace, this book is for you. The shepherds who witnessed the angelic proclamation of "good tidings of great joy" were the first to see the Prince of Peace lying in a manger. Their lives remind us that Jesus came to bring hope to the humble and light to the darkest places.

To those who seek truth, this book is for you. The wise men's journey across distant lands mirrors the call of Jesus to all who seek Him: to come, worship, and lay their treasures at His feet. Their devotion reflects the worthiness of the King who came to save us.

To those who feel small or forgotten, this book is for you. The stable, the manger, and the little town of Bethlehem—seemingly insignificant places—became the setting for the most significant event in history: the arrival of Jesus Christ. His birth reminds us that God's glory shines brightest in humility.

This book is ultimately dedicated to the One who makes Christmas a reason for joy and hope: Jesus Christ, Emmanuel—God with us. Through His birth, life, death, and resurrection, He has made a way for all of us to be part of His eternal story.

As you read, may your heart be drawn closer to the Savior. May His love, grace, and glory fill your life with awe and wonder. And may the story of Christmas, centered on Him, inspire you to worship the King who came to redeem the world.

From the moment of His miraculous birth, Jesus' life became the hinge on which all of history turns. He is the thread that weaves together the characters of Christmas—the One who called Mary to trust, Joseph to obey, shepherds to rejoice, and wise men to seek. In Him, we find our purpose, joy, and redemption.

Introduction

Day 1 - Mary
Day 2 - Joseph
Day 3 - The Shepherds
Day 4 - The Wise Men
Day 5 - Elizabeth
Day 6 - Zacharias
Day 7 - Simeon
Day 8 - Anna
Day 9 - Gabriel
Day 10 - The Heavenly Host
Day 11 - The Star
Day 12 - The Manger
Day 13 - Bethlehem
Day 14 - The Innkeeper
Day 15 - The Donkey
Day 16 - Herod
Day 17 - Caesar Augustus
Day 18 - The Stable
Day 19 - The Baby Jesus
Day 20 - The Gifts of the Wise Men
Day 21 - The Prophecies Fulfilled
Day 22 - The Journey to Bethlehem
Day 23 - The Virgin Birth
Day 24 - The Carpenter's Role
Day 25 - The Angelic Song
Day 26 - The Shepherds' Faith
Day 27 - The Gold

Introduction

The story of Christmas is more than just a moment in time—it is the weaving together of heaven and earth, the miraculous and the ordinary, to bring the greatest gift the world has ever known: Jesus Christ. It is a story filled with people whose lives were forever changed, and places that became sacred because God chose to step into them. From the quiet obedience of Mary to the faithful protection of Joseph, from the humble shepherds in their fields to the wise men traveling from afar, the characters of Christmas remind us that God uses ordinary people to accomplish His extraordinary purposes. He chose a stable over a palace, a manger over a throne, and a simple town like Bethlehem to bring forth His Son, proving that His glory shines brightest in humility. Every person in this story, every place touched by His presence, has something to teach us about God's love, His faithfulness, and His desire to be near to us. The angels proclaimed "good tidings of great joy" (Luke 2:10), and those tidings echo through the lives of the people who witnessed the first Christmas—ordinary individuals invited into an extraordinary story of redemption. Mary's faith reminds us to trust God's promises even when they seem impossible. Joseph's quiet obedience shows us the strength in surrendering to God's plan. The shepherds teach us the joy of responding to God's call, and the wise men reveal the beauty of seeking Jesus no matter the cost. Even the seemingly insignificant details—the star that guided the wise men, the manger that held the Savior, and the town of Bethlehem chosen for His birth—are reminders that God's plans are perfect, and He works through the small and overlooked to bring about His glory. In these people and places, we see ourselves, with all our doubts, fears, and hopes, invited into the wonder of God's story. The characters of Christmas are not distant figures from an ancient tale; they are reflections of the faith, hope, and love we are called to embrace today. Their lives encourage us to listen for God's voice, to step out in faith, and to open our hearts to the miraculous. As we journey through their stories, may we be reminded that the message of Christmas is not just about what happened long ago but about what God continues to do in our lives. The story of Christmas is the story of God with us—Emmanuel—and it is a story that invites us all to kneel at the manger in awe, wonder, and worship.

Day 1 - Mary

Mary, a young woman of humble origins, lived a quiet and unassuming life in Nazareth. Her days were filled with ordinary tasks—drawing water from the well, kneading dough for bread, and tending to her family. But what set Mary apart was her unwavering faith in God. She was a woman of quiet devotion, who trusted in the Lord's promises even when life was uncertain. One day, as she went about her daily routine, an angel of the Lord, Gabriel, appeared before her. His presence was overwhelming, his countenance radiant, and his words were unlike anything she had ever heard. "Hail, thou that art highly favoured, the Lord is with thee: blessed art thou among women," he said (Luke 1:28). Mary's heart trembled at the angel's greeting, but Gabriel reassured her, saying, "Fear not, Mary: for thou hast found favour with God" (Luke 1:30). The angel then revealed the extraordinary plan God had for her. She would conceive and bring forth a son, and she was to call His name Jesus. "He shall be great, and shall be called the Son of the Highest: and the Lord God shall give unto Him the throne of His father David" (Luke 1:32).

Mary, though startled, did not question God's power or wisdom. Instead, she humbly asked, "How shall this be, seeing I know not a man?" (Luke 1:34). Gabriel explained that the Holy Ghost would come upon her and that the power of the Highest would overshadow her. He also told her of her cousin Elizabeth, who, despite her old age, had conceived a son, showing that "with God nothing shall be impossible" (Luke 1:37). Mary's response was not one of doubt or hesitation but of complete surrender and faith: "Behold the handmaid of the Lord; be it unto me according to thy word" (Luke 1:38). Her acceptance of God's plan was a testament to her heart full of faith. She did not fully comprehend the magnitude of what lay ahead, but she trusted the One who had called her.

In the days that followed, Mary traveled to visit Elizabeth. Upon Mary's arrival, Elizabeth's baby leaped in her womb, and Elizabeth was filled with the Holy Ghost. She proclaimed, "Blessed art thou among women, and blessed is the fruit of thy womb" (Luke 1:42). Mary, overwhelmed by the confirmation of God's work, lifted her voice in what has become known as the Magnificat, saying, "My soul doth magnify the Lord, and my spirit hath rejoiced in God my Saviour. For He hath regarded the low estate of His handmaiden" (Luke 1:46-48). Her song of praise reflected her deep understanding of God's mercy, power, and faithfulness.

As the months passed, Mary endured the whispers and stares of those who did not understand her miraculous pregnancy. Yet, she held her head high, clinging to the angel's words and trusting that God's plan was perfect. When the decree came that all should be taxed, Mary and Joseph journeyed to Bethlehem. Despite the difficulty of traveling in her condition, Mary pressed on, her heart full of faith in the promise that she carried the Savior of the world. Upon arriving in Bethlehem, they found no room in the inn and were forced to take refuge in a stable. It was there, in the humblest of settings, that Mary gave birth to Jesus, wrapping Him in swaddling clothes and laying Him in a manger.

As Mary looked into the face of her newborn son, she marveled at the mystery of God's plan. Shepherds soon arrived, sharing the angelic message they had received: "For unto you is born this day in the city of David a Saviour, which is Christ the Lord" (Luke 2:11). Mary listened intently to their words, pondering them in her heart. She could see the hand of God moving in ways beyond her understanding, and her faith grew even stronger.

Throughout her life, Mary remained a steadfast example of faith. She stood by Jesus as He grew, taught, and performed miracles. She witnessed His suffering and death, a sword piercing her soul as Simeon had foretold (Luke 2:35). Yet, even in her darkest moments, Mary held on to the promises of God. Her faith was not rooted in her circumstances but in the unchanging character of God. Mary's story reminds us that faith is not the absence of fear or doubt but the choice to trust God in the midst of uncertainty. Her heart full of faith continues to inspire believers to say, "Be it unto me according to thy word," no matter what the cost.

Day 2 - Joseph

Joseph was a man of quiet strength and deep faith, a carpenter living in Nazareth, working each day with his hands to provide for a simple life. His days were ordinary, yet his character was extraordinary, for he was a man who sought to follow God in every decision he made. Joseph was betrothed to Mary, a young woman of pure heart and great faith, and he must have looked forward to their future together with hope and joy. But all his plans were interrupted when he discovered that Mary was with child before they had come together. This news must have shaken him to his core, filling his heart with confusion, sorrow, and the weight of uncertainty. Joseph was a righteous man, one who cared deeply for Mary, and he resolved to handle the matter with kindness, deciding to put her away privily rather than expose her to public shame. Yet in his quiet turmoil, God had a greater plan for him, a plan that would require his obedience and faith like never before.

As Joseph pondered these things, an angel of the Lord appeared to him in a dream, speaking words that would change the course of his life. "Joseph, thou son of David, fear not to take unto thee Mary thy wife: for that which is conceived in her is of the Holy Ghost. And she shall bring forth a son, and thou shalt call His name JESUS: for He shall save His people from their sins" (Matthew 1:20-21). Joseph awoke with a clarity of purpose, understanding that this was no ordinary child, but the promised Messiah, the Savior of the world. Without hesitation or doubt, Joseph obeyed the angel's command. He took Mary to be his wife, shielding her from disgrace and standing by her side with unwavering loyalty. His actions spoke volumes about his character, for Joseph was a man who did not need loud proclamations or grand gestures to prove his faith. His obedience was quiet yet powerful, grounded in trust in the God who had called him to this sacred role.

As the days unfolded, Joseph faced many challenges. The decree from Caesar Augustus forced him to take Mary, heavy with child, on the long and arduous journey to Bethlehem. He must have felt the weight of responsibility as he led the way, ensuring her safety and comfort as best as he could. Upon arriving in Bethlehem, Joseph searched tirelessly for a place where Mary could give birth, only to find no room in the inn. With resourcefulness and determination, he secured a stable, a humble and lowly place where the King of Kings would enter the world. As Mary labored, Joseph must have prayed silently, his heart full of awe and reverence for the moment unfolding before him. When Jesus was born, Joseph held the tiny baby in his arms, marveling at the miracle of God's plan. He knew that this child, so small and vulnerable, was Emmanuel, God with us.

Joseph's obedience did not end with the birth of Jesus. Shortly after, the angel of the Lord appeared to him again in a dream, warning him of Herod's wicked plot to destroy the child. "Arise, and take the young child and His mother, and flee into Egypt, and be thou there until I bring thee word: for Herod will seek the young child to destroy Him" (Matthew 2:13). Without delay, Joseph rose in the night, gathered his family, and fled to Egypt, a foreign land where he would have to start anew. His obedience was immediate and complete, showing his unwavering trust in God's guidance and his commitment to protect the Savior of the world. In Egypt, Joseph worked to provide for his family, all the while waiting for the Lord's instruction. When the angel appeared once more, telling him it was safe to return, Joseph obeyed yet again, leading his family back to the land of Israel and settling in Nazareth.

Throughout his life, Joseph's role was one of quiet yet profound significance. He was not a man who sought recognition or glory. Instead, he humbly fulfilled the tasks set before him, providing for his family, protecting the Son of God, and walking in obedience to the Lord. Joseph taught Jesus the skills of carpentry, guiding Him with patience and care, and modeling what it meant to be a man of integrity and faith. Though the Bible does not record Joseph's words, his actions speak volumes. He was a man who listened to God, who acted with courage and resolve, and who faithfully carried out the responsibilities entrusted to him. Joseph's life was a testament to the power of quiet obedience, a reminder that faithfulness in the small, unseen tasks can have eternal significance.

Even in the moments of uncertainty and fear, Joseph chose to trust God's plan. He did not question the angel's commands or seek to understand every detail. Instead, he walked forward in faith, confident that the God who had called him would provide the strength and wisdom he needed. Joseph's quiet obedience continues to inspire believers to this day, showing that true faith is not always about grand gestures or public displays but about a heart that says "yes" to God, even when the path is unclear. His story reminds us that God often works through the humble and the ordinary, using those who are willing to listen and obey to accomplish His extraordinary purposes. Joseph's legacy is one of faith, courage, and a steadfast commitment to the will of God, a legacy that points us to the ultimate act of obedience: the life, death, and resurrection of Jesus Christ. Through Joseph's quiet obedience, the Savior of the world was protected and nurtured, and God's plan of redemption was fulfilled.

Day 3 - The Shepherds

The shepherds were simple men, tending their flocks in the fields near Bethlehem under the vast canopy of the night sky. Their lives were humble, spent watching over sheep, leading them to green pastures and still waters, and protecting them from harm. They were not men of high status or wealth but ordinary individuals living ordinary lives. Yet, on one extraordinary night, the course of their lives—and the course of history—was forever changed. As they kept watch over their sheep, the quiet of the evening was suddenly interrupted by a brilliant light that pierced the darkness, a radiance so overwhelming that it caused their hearts to tremble with fear. An angel of the Lord appeared before them, his presence shining with the glory of God, and he spoke words that would echo through eternity: "Fear not: for, behold, I bring you good tidings of great joy, which shall be to all people. For unto you is born this day in the city of David a Saviour, which is Christ the Lord" (Luke 2:10-11).

The shepherds, awestruck and trembling, listened as the angel continued, describing the sign by which they would recognize the Messiah: "Ye shall find the babe wrapped in swaddling clothes, lying in a manger" (Luke 2:12). Suddenly, the night sky erupted with the voices of a multitude of the heavenly host, praising God and declaring, "Glory to God in the highest, and on earth peace, good will toward men" (Luke 2:14). The sound of their worship filled the air with a beauty and majesty that the shepherds had never known, and their hearts were overwhelmed by the divine proclamation. Then, just as suddenly as they had appeared, the angels departed, leaving the shepherds standing in stunned silence beneath the starlit sky.

Though they were men of little means and simple understanding, the shepherds knew that what they had witnessed was no ordinary event. Their fear gave way to awe, and awe gave way to action. Without hesitation, they said one to another, "Let us now go even unto Bethlehem, and see this thing which is come to pass, which the Lord hath made known unto us" (Luke 2:15). With urgency and excitement, they left their flocks and made their way to the town. Their steps were quick, their hearts pounding with anticipation, for they knew they were about to witness the fulfillment of God's promise, the arrival of the long-awaited Savior.

When they arrived in Bethlehem, they found Mary and Joseph, just as the angel had said, and there, lying in a manger, was the baby Jesus. The shepherds gazed upon Him with wonder, their rough, work-worn hands trembling as they beheld the child who was Christ the Lord. In that moment, the simplicity of the stable and the humility of the manger became a sacred scene, filled with the presence of the divine. The shepherds knelt in reverence, their hearts overflowing with gratitude and joy, for they had been chosen to witness the greatest gift ever given to mankind.

After they had seen Him, the shepherds could not keep the news to themselves. Their hearts burned with the need to share the good tidings of great joy that had been entrusted to them. As they left the stable, they made known abroad the saying which was told them concerning the child. They spoke of the angel's message, the heavenly host, and the Savior born in Bethlehem. Those who heard their words marveled at the things they told, for the message of the shepherds carried the power of truth and the joy of divine revelation. Yet, even as they shared the good news, the shepherds remained humble, for they understood that the glory belonged not to them but to God.

The shepherds returned to their flocks, glorifying and praising God for all the things that they had heard and seen, as it was told unto them (Luke 2:20). Their lives were forever changed, for they had encountered the Messiah, and their hearts had been filled with a joy that surpassed all understanding. Though they returned to the same fields and the same sheep, they were no longer the same men. The message they carried, the joy they experienced, and the faith they proclaimed were a testimony to the transforming power of the Savior's birth.

The shepherds' story is a reminder that God's message of salvation is for all people, regardless of status, wealth, or position. The Lord chose to reveal the birth of His Son not to kings or scholars but to humble shepherds, showing that His grace is available to everyone who is willing to receive it. The shepherds responded to God's call with faith and obedience, and their lives became a living proclamation of the joy and hope found in Christ. Their story encourages us to be messengers of joy in our own lives, sharing the good news of Jesus with those around us and glorifying God for the gift of His Son. Just as the shepherds experienced the wonder of that holy night, we too are invited to encounter the Savior and to carry the light of His love into a world in need of

His peace. Their faith, their joy, and their willingness to share the good news continue to inspire us to this day, reminding us that the message of Christmas is a message of hope, salvation, and everlasting joy.

Day 4 - The Wise Men

The Wise Men, known as Magi, were seekers of wisdom and truth, men of great learning and observation who studied the stars and the mysteries of the heavens. They lived in a far-off land, likely Persia or Babylon, where they poured over ancient texts and watched the skies for signs of divine activity. Though they were not Israelites, their hearts were stirred by a longing for something greater, a search for the King foretold by prophecy. One night, as they observed the stars, a remarkable event occurred: a new star appeared in the sky, radiant and unlike anything they had seen before. To the Wise Men, this was no ordinary celestial event; it was the sign of the birth of a King. They remembered the ancient words, perhaps those passed down from the time of Daniel, who had prophesied about the coming Messiah. With this revelation, they resolved to seek the child born King of the Jews, for they knew this was no earthly king but the Savior of the world.

The journey ahead was long and arduous, stretching over many miles and through unknown lands, but the Wise Men were undeterred. They gathered their treasures—gold, frankincense, and myrrh—gifts fit for a king, a priest, and one who would suffer for the sins of the world. With these precious offerings, they set out, following the star that led them westward. Day after day, night after night, they pressed on, their hearts filled with anticipation and purpose. They must have faced challenges along the way—harsh terrain, extreme weather, and the uncertainty of where their journey would end—but their faith drove them forward. They were not merely astronomers or scholars; they were men on a divine mission, guided by a God they longed to know more fully.

When the Wise Men finally arrived in Judea, they went to Jerusalem, the city of kings, assuming this would be the place to find the newborn ruler. They entered the courts of Herod, the reigning king, and asked, "Where is He that is born King of the Jews? For we have seen His star in the east, and are come to worship Him" (Matthew 2:2). Herod, a man of great ambition and paranoia, was troubled by their inquiry, for he feared the loss of his throne. He called together the chief priests and scribes, demanding to know where the Christ should be born. They answered, "In Bethlehem of Judaea: for thus it is written by the prophet" (Matthew 2:5). Herod, deceitful in his intentions, sent the

Wise Men to Bethlehem, instructing them to return with news of the child so he too could worship Him. But the Wise Men, unaware of Herod's true motives, continued their journey with hope and determination.

As they departed from Jerusalem, the star reappeared, leading them to the exact place where the child was. "When they saw the star, they rejoiced with exceeding great joy" (Matthew 2:10). Their hearts were overwhelmed with awe and gratitude, for their long journey was nearing its divine fulfillment. The star came to rest over a humble dwelling in Bethlehem, and the Wise Men entered, finding the young child with Mary, His mother. Falling to their knees, they worshiped Him, offering their treasures as tokens of their reverence and recognition of His divine identity. They presented gold, symbolizing His kingship; frankincense, representing His role as the high priest and mediator between God and man; and myrrh, foretelling His suffering and death for the salvation of humanity.

In that moment, the Wise Men, who had sought truth and wisdom their entire lives, found themselves in the presence of the source of all truth. They, men of intellect and influence, bowed before a child in humility and worship, acknowledging Him as the Savior. Their journey had led them not to a palace but to a simple home, not to a throne of gold but to a child who would reign in the hearts of men. The contrast between their expectations and the reality of God's plan must have deepened their reverence, for they understood that this King was unlike any other. He had come not to conquer by force but to save by love, not to rule over nations but to redeem souls.

After their worship, the Wise Men were warned in a dream not to return to Herod, for God revealed the king's wicked intentions. Obeying the divine warning, they departed for their own country by another route, avoiding Jerusalem and ensuring the safety of the child. Their obedience in this moment demonstrated their willingness to follow God's guidance, even at personal risk. Though their journey home was likely long and fraught with challenges, they carried with them the joy and peace of having encountered the Savior. Their lives were forever changed, for they had seen the fulfillment of their search for truth in the face of Jesus Christ.

The story of the Wise Men reminds us that God calls seekers from every nation and background. These men, who began their journey as strangers to the God of Israel, were drawn to Him through a star and a promise, showing that God's grace reaches beyond borders and boundaries. Their determination to seek the Savior, their humility in worship, and their obedience to divine direction are a powerful example of what it means to pursue God with all our hearts. The Wise Men teach us that the journey to Christ may not always be easy or straightforward, but it is always worth it. They sought the Savior with faith and found in Him the fulfillment of their deepest longings.

As we reflect on the Wise Men's journey, we are challenged to consider our own pursuit of the Savior. Are we willing to seek Him with the same diligence and devotion, to offer Him our most precious treasures, and to bow before Him in worship? Their story calls us to lay aside our pride and preconceived notions, to trust in God's leading, and to rejoice in the discovery of His Son. The Wise Men's journey is a timeless testament to the truth that those who seek the Savior will find Him, for He is faithful to reveal Himself to all who earnestly search for Him. Their legacy encourages us to be seekers of the Savior, messengers of His joy, and worshippers of His glory, pointing others to the One who is the light of the world and the King of kings.

Day 5 - Elizabeth

Elizabeth was a woman who lived a life marked by quiet faithfulness, steadfast prayer, and unwavering hope, even in the face of years of unfulfilled longing. She was a descendant of Aaron, the priestly line, and her husband, Zacharias, served as a priest in the temple of the Lord. Together, they were righteous before God, walking in all the commandments and ordinances of the Lord blameless (Luke 1:6). Yet, for all their devotion, Elizabeth bore the deep sorrow of barrenness, a condition that in her time was often seen as a reproach. She carried this burden in silence, her heart aching for the joy of a child, yet she never let it diminish her trust in God. Though the years passed and her hope seemed beyond reach, Elizabeth remained faithful, her life a testament to patience and quiet grace.

One day, as Zacharias performed his priestly duties in the temple, offering incense before the Lord, an angel of the Lord appeared to him. Fear gripped Zacharias, but the angel spoke words that would change both their lives forever: "Fear not, Zacharias: for thy prayer is heard; and thy wife Elizabeth shall bear thee a son, and thou shalt call his name John" (Luke 1:13). The angel described the child's extraordinary purpose, that he would be great in the sight of the Lord, filled with the Holy Ghost even from his mother's womb, and would turn many of the children of Israel to the Lord their God (Luke 1:15-16). But Zacharias, overcome with doubt because of their old age, questioned the angel's message and was struck dumb as a sign until the prophecy would come to pass.

When Zacharias returned home, Elizabeth soon conceived, just as the angel had foretold. Her heart overflowed with gratitude and wonder at the Lord's mercy. She said, "Thus hath the Lord dealt with me in the days wherein He looked on me, to take away my reproach among men" (Luke 1:25). Elizabeth recognized that this miraculous blessing was not merely an answer to her personal longing but a part of God's grand plan of redemption. Her life, once overshadowed by sorrow, was now filled with the joy of carrying a child destined to prepare the way for the Messiah.

As her pregnancy progressed, Elizabeth experienced a second miraculous visitation, this time from her young relative Mary. Mary had also received a divine message from the angel Gabriel, announcing that she would conceive by the Holy Ghost and bear the Son of God. When Mary entered Elizabeth's home and greeted her, something extraordinary happened: the baby in Elizabeth's womb leaped for joy, and Elizabeth was filled with the Holy Ghost (Luke 1:41). In that moment, Elizabeth spoke words of prophecy and blessing over Mary, saying, "Blessed art thou among women, and blessed is the fruit of thy womb. And whence is this to me, that the mother of my Lord should come to me?" (Luke 1:42-43). Elizabeth's words were not only an acknowledgment of Mary's role but also a profound affirmation of the child Mary carried, the long-awaited Messiah. Her humility and joy in this moment revealed her deep understanding of God's grace and her willingness to rejoice in His plan, even as it unfolded through others.

Elizabeth's life continued to be marked by God's grace as she carried John, a child who would be known as John the Baptist, the forerunner of Christ. When the time came for her to give birth, her neighbors and relatives rejoiced with her, marveling at the great mercy the Lord had shown her. On the eighth day, when the child was to be named, those gathered expected him to be called after his father, Zacharias. But Elizabeth, with quiet confidence, declared, "Not so; but he shall be called John" (Luke 1:60). Her words reflected her obedience to the angel's instruction, even in the face of societal expectations. When Zacharias confirmed the name by writing, "His name is John," his tongue was loosed, and he began to praise God (Luke 1:63-64).

Elizabeth's life, though often in the background of the biblical narrative, is a powerful example of how God's grace works through faithfulness, patience, and humility. She endured years of waiting and disappointment, yet she never turned away from the Lord. Her faith was rewarded not only with the gift of a son but with the knowledge that her child would play a pivotal role in God's redemptive plan. Elizabeth's story reminds us that God's timing is perfect, even when it feels delayed, and that His blessings often exceed our greatest hopes.

In Elizabeth's later years, she would have watched as her son John grew into the prophet he was destined to be, calling the people to repentance and preparing their hearts for the coming of Jesus. Her influence as a mother, her prayers, and her steadfast example surely shaped John's early life, grounding him in the knowledge of God's purpose and grace. Though her name may not be as prominent as others in Scripture, Elizabeth's life shines as a testament to the power of God's faithfulness and the beauty of a heart that trusts in His plan.

Elizabeth's story calls us to live lives of quiet faith, trusting that God sees our struggles, hears our prayers, and works all things for His glory and our good. Her humility, her joy in others' blessings, and her unwavering obedience inspire us to embrace God's grace in every season of life. Even when the wait is long, even when the path is uncertain, we can look to Elizabeth as a model of what it means to live a life blessed by grace—a life that finds its fulfillment not in earthly recognition but in the faithfulness of the God who calls and redeems. Through Elizabeth, we see the beauty of a life fully surrendered to the Lord, a life that rejoices in His goodness and trusts in His perfect will.

Day 6 - Zacharias

Zacharias, a priest of the course of Abia, was a man of devotion, a servant of the Lord who walked in righteousness, keeping all the commandments and ordinances of God blamelessly. He and his wife, Elizabeth, shared a bond of faith and love, yet their lives carried the sorrow of unfulfilled longing. They were childless, and now advanced in years, their hopes of becoming parents had faded into the past. The ache of barrenness weighed heavily on their hearts, a silent burden they bore with quiet endurance. Despite their personal pain, Zacharias faithfully carried out his priestly duties, serving in the temple of the Lord. One day, as he stood before the altar of incense, performing the sacred ritual, the angel of the Lord appeared to him, standing on the right side of the altar. Fear gripped Zacharias at the sight, but the angel spoke words of reassurance and divine promise: "Fear not, Zacharias: for thy prayer is heard; and thy wife Elizabeth shall bear thee a son, and thou shalt call his name John" (Luke 1:13).

The angel's message was filled with wonder and prophecy. This child, John, would not be an ordinary boy but a prophet of the Most High, one who would be filled with the Holy Ghost even from his mother's womb and would turn many of the children of Israel to the Lord their God (Luke 1:15-16). He would go before the Messiah in the spirit and power of Elias, preparing the hearts of the people for the coming of the Lord. But Zacharias, overwhelmed by the angel's words and the weight of his doubts, questioned the promise: "Whereby shall I know this? for I am an old man, and my wife well stricken in years" (Luke 1:18). The angel, revealing himself as Gabriel, who stands in the presence of God, declared that because of Zacharias's unbelief, he would be struck silent, unable to speak until the day the promise was fulfilled.

When Zacharias emerged from the temple, his inability to speak astonished the people, who perceived that he had seen a vision. From that moment, silence became his constant companion, a daily reminder of the power of God's word and the importance of faith. Though he could not express his thoughts, Zacharias surely reflected deeply on the angel's message, pondering the miracle that was unfolding in his life. He watched as Elizabeth conceived, her joy and gratitude filling their home with hope and anticipation.

In his silence, Zacharias began to see the hand of God moving in ways beyond human understanding, and his heart was being prepared for the song that would one day burst forth from his lips.

As Elizabeth's pregnancy progressed, the arrival of her young relative Mary brought another layer of wonder. Mary, too, carried a divine promise, for she was chosen to bear the Son of God. When Mary greeted Elizabeth, the baby in Elizabeth's womb leaped for joy, and Elizabeth, filled with the Holy Ghost, proclaimed the greatness of the Lord. Zacharias, though silent, witnessed this moment of divine confirmation, understanding that his son would play a vital role in the unfolding plan of redemption. The months passed, and the time came for Elizabeth to give birth. When their son was born, the neighbors and relatives rejoiced with them, marveling at the great mercy the Lord had shown. On the eighth day, during the circumcision ceremony, the moment came to name the child. The people assumed he would be named after his father, but Elizabeth declared, "Not so; but he shall be called John" (Luke 1:60). Confused, they turned to Zacharias for confirmation.

In that pivotal moment, Zacharias, who had been unable to speak for months, took a writing tablet and wrote, "His name is John" (Luke 1:63). Immediately, his tongue was loosed, and his first words were not of complaint or regret but of praise and worship. He was filled with the Holy Ghost and began to prophesy, declaring the greatness of God and the fulfillment of His promises. "Blessed be the Lord God of Israel; for He hath visited and redeemed His people, and hath raised up an horn of salvation for us in the house of His servant David" (Luke 1:68-69). Zacharias's song, often called the Benedictus, was a hymn of thanksgiving and prophecy. He spoke of God's covenant with Abraham, the deliverance of His people, and the light that would shine upon those who sit in darkness, guiding their feet into the way of peace (Luke 1:79).

In his song, Zacharias also spoke directly about his son, John, declaring his role as the prophet of the Highest, who would go before the face of the Lord to prepare His ways and give knowledge of salvation to His people by the remission of their sins (Luke 1:76-77). Zacharias's words were not merely a father's pride but the Spirit-filled proclamation of God's divine purpose for his child. In this moment, the silence that had once been a consequence of doubt became a testimony of grace, transforming into a song of faith and hope.

Zacharias's story is a powerful reminder of the transformative power of God's grace. His initial doubt, though met with discipline, was not the end of his story. In his silence, God worked within him, teaching him to trust in the promises of the Lord. When the time came for him to speak, his words were a reflection of a heart that had been humbled and renewed by the grace of God. His journey from silence to song reminds us that even in our moments of doubt and weakness, God is patient and faithful, working all things for His glory.

Through Zacharias, we see the importance of waiting on the Lord and trusting in His timing. His months of silence were not wasted but were a season of preparation, allowing him to witness the unfolding of God's plan with awe and reverence. When his voice was restored, it was not to reclaim his own authority but to magnify the Lord and proclaim His faithfulness. Zacharias's story encourages us to reflect on our own moments of silence, whether they are seasons of waiting, doubt, or struggle, and to trust that God is working within us to bring forth a song of praise in His perfect time.

Zacharias's song, born out of his encounter with the divine and the fulfillment of God's promise, continues to inspire believers to this day. It reminds us of the faithfulness of God, the joy of His redemption, and the hope of His salvation. Through Zacharias, we learn that silence is not the absence of God but often a space where He prepares us for something greater. His life, his silence, and his song point us to the ultimate fulfillment of God's promise in Jesus Christ, the Savior who came to redeem and restore us to Himself.

Day 7 - Simeon

Simeon was a man of deep faith and steadfast hope, living in Jerusalem at a time when darkness seemed to overshadow the land. The Roman Empire ruled with an iron hand, and many among the people of Israel had grown weary of waiting for the promised Messiah. Yet Simeon's heart was not weighed down by despair, for he lived in constant anticipation of the fulfillment of God's word. The Scriptures tell us that Simeon was a just and devout man, waiting for the consolation of Israel, and the Holy Ghost was upon him (Luke 2:25). He was not a man of wealth or great influence but a humble servant of God who dedicated his life to prayer, worship, and unwavering faith. Simeon had been given a unique promise by the Holy Ghost, one that set him apart from others in his time. It had been revealed to him that he would not see death before he had seen the Lord's Christ (Luke 2:26). This divine assurance became the anchor of his soul, a light that guided him through the uncertainties and trials of life, giving him purpose and hope.

Day after day, Simeon waited and watched, his heart attuned to the voice of the Spirit. He would often go to the temple, the sacred place where God's presence dwelled, seeking solace in prayer and worship, his eyes scanning the crowds with the hope that today might be the day he would behold the Savior. Though the years passed and his body grew frail with age, Simeon's faith did not waver. He clung to the promise of God, trusting that the One who had spoken would be faithful to fulfill His word. Simeon's life was marked by quiet perseverance, a testament to the power of patient faith. In a world that often rushed past him, Simeon stood as a watchful witness, his heart fixed on the eternal.

Then, one ordinary day, the extraordinary happened. Simeon, led by the Spirit, went into the temple. As he entered, a young couple walked in, carrying an infant in their arms. They were Mary and Joseph, and the child they held was Jesus, the Messiah, though to most onlookers, they seemed no different from the many families who came to present their firstborns to the Lord. But Simeon, guided by the Holy Ghost, recognized the divine nature of the child. His heart must have leaped within him as he approached Mary and Joseph, his eyes fixed on the baby who was the fulfillment of all he had hoped for, prayed for, and waited for. With trembling hands, he took the child into his arms, and in that sacred moment, Simeon's faith became sight.

Lifting his voice in praise, Simeon declared, "Lord, now lettest Thou Thy servant depart in peace, according to Thy word: For mine eyes have seen Thy salvation, which Thou hast prepared before the face of all people; a light to lighten the Gentiles, and the glory of Thy people Israel" (Luke 2:29-32). His words, known as the Nunc Dimittis, were a song of fulfillment and gratitude. Simeon's heart overflowed with joy and peace, for he had seen the salvation of the Lord, not in the form of a conquering king but in the innocence of a newborn child. He recognized that this child, Jesus, was not just the hope of Israel but the hope of the entire world—a light to the Gentiles and the glory of God's chosen people.

As Simeon held the child, he blessed Mary and Joseph, but his words were not without a note of solemnity. Turning to Mary, he said, "Behold, this child is set for the fall and rising again of many in Israel; and for a sign which shall be spoken against; (Yea, a sword shall pierce through thy own soul also,) that the thoughts of many hearts may be revealed" (Luke 2:34-35). Simeon's prophecy was both a celebration of the Messiah's arrival and a foreshadowing of the suffering that would come. He saw that Jesus would be a dividing line, revealing the true nature of the hearts of men, and he warned Mary of the deep sorrow she would experience as the mother of the Savior. Simeon's words, though heavy, were spoken with the clarity and conviction of one who had been in the presence of God.

In Simeon's story, we see a portrait of what it means to live a life of faith and expectation. He was a man who trusted in the promises of God, even when they seemed distant or delayed. His watchfulness and obedience to the Spirit allowed him to recognize the Messiah when others might have overlooked Him. Simeon's encounter with Jesus was the culmination of a lifetime of devotion, a moment that affirmed his faith and fulfilled his hope. His song of praise reminds us that God's promises are sure and that His salvation is for all people, regardless of status, nationality, or background.

Simeon's life challenges us to consider our own posture of faith. Are we watchful like Simeon, attuned to the Spirit's leading, and patient in our waiting for the fulfillment of God's promises? Do we trust that God's timing is perfect, even when it does not align with our own? Simeon's example encourages us to keep our eyes fixed on Jesus, the author and finisher of our faith, and to live with the hope and expectation that He will fulfill every word He has spoken.

As Simeon departed the temple that day, his heart was at peace, for he had seen the salvation of the Lord. Though we do not know the details of his life beyond this moment, his legacy as a watchful witness endures. He reminds us that faith is not about instant gratification but about trusting in the faithfulness of God. Through Simeon, we see that God's promises are worth the wait and that the joy of encountering the Savior far outweighs the trials of the journey. His story invites us to join him in lifting our voices in praise, declaring with him that our eyes have seen God's salvation, a light to the Gentiles, and the glory of His people Israel.

Day 8 - Anna

Anna was a woman whose life was a portrait of devotion, faith, and unceasing worship. Living in Jerusalem during a time of great spiritual longing, Anna stood apart as one wholly dedicated to God. She was a prophetess, the daughter of Phanuel, of the tribe of Asher, and she carried a lineage that traced back to the people of Israel's rich heritage. Her story, though brief in the Scriptures, is profoundly moving, showing the strength of a heart fully given to God. Married in her youth, Anna's joy as a bride was short-lived, for she was widowed after just seven years of marriage. Left without the companionship of her husband, Anna could have allowed sorrow to consume her life, but instead, she turned her heart wholly toward the Lord. The temple became her home, a sacred place where she worshiped day and night with fasting and prayer (Luke 2:37).

Anna's life was not marked by worldly pursuits or the comforts that others might have sought in her circumstances. Instead, it was defined by her single-minded devotion to God. For decades, she remained steadfast, her heart fixed on the promises of Scripture and the hope of the coming Messiah. The years of waiting were not idle but were filled with fervent prayer, continual worship, and a faith that only deepened with time. Anna's dedication to the temple was not out of obligation but out of love, a love for the God who had sustained her through loss and loneliness. Her life was a testament to the beauty of worship, a life lived not for the fleeting things of earth but for the eternal glory of God.

As the years turned into decades, Anna's faith did not waver. Though she had witnessed the struggles of her people under Roman rule and the spiritual barrenness that weighed heavily on Israel, Anna's hope remained unshaken. She clung to the promises of God, trusting that He would send the Redeemer who had been foretold by the prophets. Her life of worship became a beacon of hope for those around her, a reminder that God is faithful and His timing is perfect. Even in her old age, Anna's spirit was vibrant with the joy of the Lord, her eyes lifted to heaven in expectation of the day when the Messiah would come.

Then, one day, the promise she had long awaited was fulfilled. Led by the Spirit, Anna entered the temple at the very moment Mary and Joseph brought the infant Jesus to present Him to the Lord. As she saw the child, her heart must have leaped with a joy that words could scarcely contain. This was the One she had prayed for, fasted for, and longed to see—the Messiah, the Savior of the world. Though He was but a baby in His mother's arms, Anna recognized Him as the fulfillment of God's promise, the light that would shine upon all nations. Her eyes, dimmed by age but bright with faith, beheld the child, and her soul overflowed with praise.

Anna's response was immediate and profound. She lifted her voice in thanksgiving to God, her worship pouring out in a song of gratitude and awe. She spoke of the child to all who looked for redemption in Jerusalem, proclaiming the good news that the Savior had come (Luke 2:38). Anna's words were not just the utterances of an elderly woman but the testimony of a prophetess whose life had been shaped by divine purpose. She became a messenger of hope, her voice echoing through the temple courts as she shared the joy of the Messiah's arrival with all who would listen.

Her encounter with Jesus was the culmination of a lifetime of worship, a moment that validated every prayer, every fast, and every tear she had shed in faith. Anna's story is a reminder that God sees the faithful, hears their prayers, and rewards those who diligently seek Him. Her life, though seemingly ordinary to the world, was extraordinary in the eyes of God. She exemplifies the truth that worship is not confined to moments of music or ceremony but is a life lived in surrender and devotion to the Lord.

Anna's story challenges us to consider the focus of our own lives. Are we, like Anna, willing to lay aside the distractions of the world to fix our hearts on God? Do we persist in prayer and worship, even when the wait feels long or the answers seem distant? Anna teaches us that a lifetime of worship is not about perfection but about perseverance, about showing up day after day with a heart that says, "Lord, I trust You, and I am here to seek You." Her life inspires us to cultivate a faith that does not falter, a hope that does not fade, and a love for God that grows stronger with each passing year.

Through Anna, we see that God's promises are worth the wait and that His timing is always perfect. Her decades of worship prepared her heart to recognize the Savior, and her joy in that moment was a reflection of a life lived in the presence of God. Anna's story is a beautiful reminder that no season of life is wasted when it is surrendered to the Lord. Whether in the joys of youth, the trials of loss, or the quiet years of waiting, God is at work, shaping us and drawing us closer to Himself.

As Anna departed the temple that day, her heart was surely filled with peace, for she had seen the salvation of the Lord. Though her name appears only briefly in Scripture, her legacy of worship and faith endures, inspiring generations to seek the Lord with all their hearts. Anna's life was a song of praise, a light in the darkness, and a testimony to the power of a heart wholly given to God. Her story reminds us that true worship is not about what we do for God but about who we become as we dwell in His presence. Through Anna, we are invited to live lives of worship, lifting our eyes to heaven in faith and lifting our voices in praise, trusting that the God who fulfilled His promise to her will be faithful to fulfill His promises to us.

Day 9 - Gabriel

GABRIEL, THE MIGHTY messenger of God, stands as one of the most awe-inspiring figures in Scripture, a being whose very presence declares the power and glory of the Almighty. Known as an angel who stands in the presence of God (Luke 1:19), Gabriel's role throughout the Bible is one of profound significance, carrying messages that change the course of history and unveil God's divine plan for humanity. Whenever Gabriel appears, the ordinary is transformed into the extraordinary, for he is the herald of good news, chosen to deliver words of hope, redemption, and the fulfillment of God's promises. His name, meaning "God is my strength," reflects the source of his power and purpose, for he serves not by his own will but as an instrument of the Lord's divine will, bringing messages of eternal significance to a world in need of salvation.

Gabriel first appears in Scripture during the time of Daniel, centuries before the birth of Christ. Daniel, a man beloved of God and known for his steadfast faith, had been seeking understanding through prayer and fasting when Gabriel was sent to him. As Gabriel approached, Daniel was overwhelmed by the angel's radiant presence and fell trembling to the ground. Gabriel's words were filled with authority and clarity as he revealed God's plans for the future, including the timeline for the coming of the Messiah (Daniel 9:21-27). His message was not merely a vision for Daniel but a promise that echoed through the ages, offering hope to a world waiting for the Deliverer. Gabriel's role in Daniel's life established him as a bearer of divine revelation, one whose words carried the weight of eternity.

Centuries later, Gabriel was sent again, this time to an aging priest named Zacharias. As Zacharias stood in the temple, burning incense before the Lord, Gabriel appeared beside the altar, his presence shining with the glory of heaven. Zacharias was struck with fear, but Gabriel spoke words of reassurance: "Fear not, Zacharias: for thy prayer is heard; and thy wife Elizabeth shall bear thee a son, and thou shalt call his name John" (Luke 1:13). The message was astounding, for Elizabeth was barren, and both she and Zacharias were well advanced in years. Gabriel explained that their son, John, would be no ordinary child but the forerunner of the Messiah, filled with the Holy Ghost even from his mother's womb and destined to prepare the hearts of the people for the Lord (Luke 1:15-17). Though Zacharias doubted, questioning how such a thing could be, Gabriel's response was firm and unwavering: "I am Gabriel, that stand in the presence of God; and am sent to speak unto thee, and to shew thee these glad tidings" (Luke 1:19). Because of Zacharias's unbelief, Gabriel declared that he would be struck mute until the promise was fulfilled, a powerful reminder of the authority and truth of God's word.

Gabriel's most well-known appearance came six months later when he was sent to a small town in Galilee called Nazareth. There, he appeared to a young virgin named Mary, a humble and devout woman engaged to a carpenter named Joseph. As Gabriel greeted her, saying, "Hail, thou that art highly favoured, the Lord is with thee: blessed art thou among women" (Luke 1:28), Mary was troubled, unsure of what manner of salutation this might be. Sensing her fear, Gabriel reassured her with words of comfort and revelation: "Fear not, Mary: for thou hast found favour with God. And, behold, thou shalt conceive in thy womb, and bring forth a son, and shalt call His name JESUS" (Luke 1:30-31). Gabriel went on to describe the nature of this child, declaring, "He shall be great, and shall be called the Son of the Highest: and the Lord God shall give unto Him the throne of His father David: and He shall reign over the house of Jacob for ever; and of His kingdom there shall be no end" (Luke 1:32-33).

Mary, though awestruck by the magnitude of Gabriel's message, responded with faith, asking only how such a thing could happen since she was a virgin. Gabriel explained that the Holy Ghost would come upon her and the power of the Highest would overshadow her, ensuring that the child born of her would be called the Son of God (Luke 1:35). As further reassurance, he told her of her cousin Elizabeth's miraculous pregnancy, declaring, "For with God nothing shall be impossible" (Luke 1:37). Mary's response, "Behold the handmaid of the Lord; be it unto me according to thy word" (Luke 1:38), was a testament to her faith and submission, and with that, Gabriel departed, his mission accomplished.

Gabriel's role in the events leading up to the birth of Christ was unparalleled, for he delivered messages that revealed the very heart of God's redemptive plan. Each time he appeared, his words brought not only revelation but also transformation, challenging those who heard them to respond in faith and obedience. Gabriel's announcements were not just for the individuals to whom he spoke but for all humanity, for they declared the coming of the Savior who would bring salvation and light to a world in darkness. His words carried the authority of heaven, and his presence was a reminder that God's promises are sure and His timing is perfect.

Through Gabriel, we see the faithfulness of God in sending His message of hope and salvation to those who needed it most. Whether speaking to a prophet seeking understanding, an aging priest longing for a child, or a young virgin chosen to bear the Son of God, Gabriel's mission was always the same: to proclaim the good news of God's plan and to prepare the way for its fulfillment. His life as an angelic messenger reminds us that God is always at work, even in the moments when we cannot see it, and that His word is powerful and unchanging.

Gabriel's story also challenges us to consider how we respond to the messages God brings into our lives. Do we, like Mary, receive them with faith and submission, trusting in His power to accomplish what He has promised? Or do we, like Zacharias, doubt, forgetting that with God, nothing is impossible? Gabriel's unwavering commitment to his role as a messenger of God encourages us to be faithful in sharing the good news of Christ with others, proclaiming His love and salvation to a world in need.

As we reflect on Gabriel's appearances in Scripture, we are reminded that his message is still relevant today. The good news he proclaimed—the coming of the Savior, the fulfillment of God's promises, and the power of His redemption—is the foundation of our faith and the hope of our salvation. Gabriel's life as a herald of good news points us to the ultimate Messenger, Jesus Christ, who came to reveal the love of the Father and to bring us into a relationship with Him. Through Gabriel, we see the beauty of a life lived in obedience to God's calling and the power of words spoken in truth and love. His story inspires us to live as heralds of the gospel, carrying the message of Christ to all who will hear and declaring with boldness and joy the glad tidings of great joy that are for all people.

Day 10 - The Heavenly Host

The night was quiet, the fields near Bethlehem bathed in the silver light of the stars, as shepherds kept watch over their flocks. It seemed like any other night, ordinary and still, until suddenly, the sky was torn open by a glory that no words could fully describe. The heavens were ablaze with a light so radiant it caused the shepherds to fall to their knees in fear, for they had never witnessed anything so wondrous. An angel of the Lord appeared to them, his presence glowing with the glory of God, and he spoke words that would forever change their lives: "Fear not: for, behold, I bring you good tidings of great joy, which shall be to all people. For unto you is born this day in the city of David a Saviour, which is Christ the Lord" (Luke 2:10-11). The angel's voice carried the promise of hope, peace, and salvation, and as the shepherds listened, their fear began to melt away, replaced by awe and wonder. But the angel was not alone in his proclamation. As he finished speaking, the heavens erupted in praise, and a multitude of the heavenly host appeared, filling the sky with a sound unlike any other.

The heavenly host, an army of angels, stood as the singers of peace, their voices lifted in perfect harmony, declaring the glory of God and the promise of His salvation. "Glory to God in the highest, and on earth peace, good will toward men" (Luke 2:14). Their song was not merely beautiful but powerful, a proclamation that resonated through the heavens and the earth, echoing across time and space. It was a declaration that the long-awaited Messiah, the

Prince of Peace, had come to bring reconciliation between God and man. The angels, who had witnessed the majesty of creation and the sorrow of the fall, now celebrated the beginning of redemption, for the birth of Jesus marked the turning point in God's plan to save humanity.

Each note of their song was filled with meaning, a testimony to the love and grace of the Creator. They sang of God's glory, lifting His name above all else, for the birth of Christ was the ultimate demonstration of His power and mercy. They sang of peace, a peace that could not be found in the world's fleeting pleasures or in the rule of earthly kings but only in the Savior who had come to reconcile sinful humanity with a holy God. They sang of goodwill toward men, a message of hope that extended to all people, regardless of their status, background, or nationality. The angels' song was a divine invitation, calling all who heard it to enter into the joy of the Lord and to embrace the gift of salvation.

The heavenly host, though mighty and magnificent, did not draw attention to themselves but pointed all glory to God. Their song was not about their power or beauty but about the greatness of the One who had sent them. They rejoiced in the fulfillment of God's promises, for they had seen His faithfulness throughout history and now beheld the culmination of His plan in the form of a tiny baby lying in a manger. The angels understood what many on earth could not yet grasp—that this child, born in the humblest of settings, was the Savior of the world, the Lamb of God who would take away the sin of the world. Their song was a celebration of God's love, a love so great that He sent His only begotten Son to dwell among men, to live and die for their redemption.

The shepherds, though ordinary men, were privileged to witness this heavenly chorus, and their hearts were forever changed. As the angels sang, the shepherds must have felt the weight of their message, the reality of God's presence, and the wonder of His grace. The heavenly host, with their voices lifted in praise, became the first messengers of the gospel, proclaiming the good news of Christ's birth to a world in desperate need of hope. Their song, though sung over two thousand years ago, still resonates today, reminding us of the peace that comes through Jesus Christ and the joy of knowing Him as our Savior.

The appearance of the heavenly host also reminds us of the spiritual reality that surrounds us. Though unseen, the angels are ever present, ministering to God's people and carrying out His will. On that night in Bethlehem, the veil between heaven and earth was momentarily lifted, allowing the shepherds to see the glory of the heavenly realm and to hear the voices of those who continually worship God. The angels, who had longed to look into the mysteries of salvation (1 Peter 1:12), now rejoiced at its unfolding, their song a reflection of the eternal praise that fills the courts of heaven.

The heavenly host challenges us to lift our own voices in worship, to join in their song of glory and peace. Their message calls us to give glory to God in all that we do, to seek the peace that comes through Christ, and to share His goodwill with others. The angels' song is not just a historical moment but a timeless truth, a reminder that the birth of Jesus is the greatest gift the world has ever known. Through their example, we are encouraged to fix our eyes on the Savior, to let our lives be a reflection of His love, and to proclaim His name with boldness and joy.

The heavenly host, the singers of peace, stand as a testament to the power of worship and the beauty of God's plan. Their song, simple yet profound, continues to inspire and transform hearts, pointing us to the One who is the source of all peace and the fulfillment of all hope. As we reflect on their message, we are reminded that the good news they proclaimed is still true today—that Jesus Christ has come to save us, to bring us peace, and to reconcile us to God. Through the heavenly host, we catch a glimpse of the glory of heaven and are invited to join in their eternal song, lifting our voices in praise to the One who is worthy of all honor, glory, and praise. Their song echoes across the ages, calling us to remember the miracle of that holy night and to rejoice in the Savior who brings peace on earth and goodwill toward men.

Day 11 - The Star

The star, shining brightly in the night sky over Bethlehem, was more than just a celestial phenomenon; it was a divine beacon of hope, a guiding light sent by God to announce the birth of His Son and to lead seekers to the Savior of the world. From the moment it appeared, the star captured the attention of those who gazed at the heavens, its brilliance a stark contrast to the darkness of the world. It was a star unlike any other, placed by the Creator Himself, shining with purpose and proclaiming the fulfillment of ancient prophecies. The wise men, learned scholars and observers of the skies, saw this extraordinary star in the east and understood its significance. They knew it was the sign of a king, a ruler whose reign would bring peace and salvation, not only to Israel but to all nations. Their hearts were stirred with a longing to find this King, and they began their journey, following the star that would lead them to the one born King of the Jews.

The star, steadfast and unwavering, became their guide, illuminating the path through foreign lands and uncertain terrain. Night after night, it shone above them, a constant reminder of the promise that lay ahead. Though the journey was long and the challenges many, the star remained their compass, filling their hearts with hope and anticipation. It was not a fleeting light but a steady presence, leading them closer to the fulfillment of their search. The wise men's journey was one of faith, for they had not seen the King, yet they believed the message of the star and trusted that it would bring them to Him. The star was more than a guide for their feet; it was a beacon of hope for their souls, a reminder that God's promises are true and His timing is perfect.

As they traveled, the wise men must have pondered the significance of the star and the King it announced. They were men of knowledge and understanding, familiar with the ancient prophecies of a Messiah who would bring light to a darkened world. The star confirmed what their hearts already longed for—a Savior who would bring hope to the hopeless, peace to the restless, and joy to the sorrowful. Each step of their journey brought them closer to the fulfillment of this hope, and the star remained a faithful guide, shining brightly against the vast expanse of the night sky. It was a light that could not be ignored, a divine signal that the time had come for God's greatest gift to be revealed to the world.

When the wise men arrived in Jerusalem, they began to inquire, saying, "Where is He that is born King of the Jews? For we have seen His star in the east, and are come to worship Him" (Matthew 2:2). Their words caused a stir, for the people of Jerusalem, and even King Herod himself, were troubled by the news of a newborn King. Herod, fearing the loss of his throne, sought to deceive the wise men, asking them to bring him word of the child so that he, too, might worship Him. But the wise men's true purpose was to find the child and offer their worship to Him alone. As they departed Jerusalem, the star appeared once again, leading them with precision and clarity. "When they saw the star, they rejoiced with exceeding great joy" (Matthew 2:10). Their joy was a reflection of the hope that had sustained them throughout their journey, a hope that was now becoming reality.

The star led them to Bethlehem, to the very place where the child was. Its light came to rest over the house where Mary and Joseph lived, and there, in the presence of the young child, the wise men fell to their knees in worship. They presented their treasures—gold, a gift fit for a king; frankincense, a symbol of worship and prayer; and myrrh, a prophetic gift foretelling the sacrifice the child would one day make. The star had fulfilled its purpose, guiding these seekers to the Savior, the light of the world, who had come to bring hope and salvation to all people. In that moment, the wise men's journey of faith reached its culmination, and the star's light was a testament to the faithfulness of God.

The star was not just a guide for the wise men but a symbol of hope for all humanity. It announced the arrival of the Messiah, the light of the world who came to dispel the darkness of sin and bring redemption to all who would believe. Its brilliance was a reminder that God's promises are sure, and its steady presence declared that He is faithful to lead those who seek Him. The star's light, though it shone in a specific time and place, continues to shine in the hearts of those who look to Jesus, the true light who gives hope to the hopeless and life to the weary.

The story of the star challenges us to follow the light of Christ in our own lives. Just as the wise men trusted the star to lead them to the Savior, we are called to trust Jesus, the light of the world, to guide us through the uncertainties and trials of life. The star reminds us that God's light is always present, even in the darkest of times, and that His guidance is sure for those who seek Him with all their hearts. It invites us to lift our eyes to heaven, to look beyond the distractions of the world, and to fix our gaze on the One who brings eternal hope and peace.

As we reflect on the star, we are reminded of the faithfulness of God, who sent His Son into the world to be a beacon of hope for all people. The star's light points us to Jesus, the source of all hope, and calls us to worship Him as the wise men did, offering our hearts and lives as gifts to the King of kings. The star, a simple yet profound symbol, continues to inspire us to follow the light of Christ, to trust in His promises, and to rejoice in the hope that He brings. Its brilliance reminds us that the same God who placed the star in the sky to guide the wise men is still at work in our lives, leading us to the Savior and filling our hearts with His peace and joy. Through the story of the star, we are invited to embark on our own journey of faith, to seek the Savior with all our hearts, and to rejoice in the hope that only He can bring.

Day 12 - The Manger

The manger, a simple wooden feeding trough, stood in a lowly stable in Bethlehem, surrounded by the earthy smells of hay and animals. It was not a place of grandeur or splendor, not a setting for kings or royalty, yet on the night of Christ's birth, it became the most sacred of thrones. This humble manger cradled the King of Kings, the Lord of Lords, the Savior of the world, and in its simplicity, it spoke of a God who chose to enter His creation not in power and majesty but in humility and grace. The manger, rough and ordinary, was transformed by the presence of the Holy Child, the eternal Word made flesh, who came to dwell among us (John 1:14). It was a throne unlike any other, for it declared a message of love that reached to the lowliest of places, inviting all to come and see the One who would bring salvation to the world.

On that holy night, the cries of a newborn pierced the stillness, and Mary, with trembling hands and a heart full of wonder, wrapped her baby in swaddling clothes and laid Him in the manger (Luke 2:7). The child, so small and vulnerable, was Emmanuel, God with us, the fulfillment of centuries of prophecy. The prophet Isaiah had foretold His coming, saying, "For unto us a child is born, unto us a son is given: and the government shall be upon His shoulder: and His name shall be called Wonderful, Counsellor, The mighty God, The everlasting Father, The Prince of Peace" (Isaiah 9:6). Yet, instead of a palace or a golden crib, this promised Savior began His earthly life in the simplest of places, surrounded by the humblest of circumstances. The manger was a symbol of His mission, a declaration that His kingdom was not of this world (John 18:36) and that His love extended to all, regardless of status or wealth.

The stable was not adorned with riches or grandeur, but it was filled with the beauty of God's presence. The animals, unaware of the significance of the moment, stood silently as the Creator of the universe entered the world He had made. The straw that lined the manger cradled the One who would one day carry the weight of the cross, and the wooden beams that supported the stable foreshadowed the wood of the tree on which He would give His life for humanity. The manger, though humble and lowly, was a throne of grace, for it held the One who would reign not through force but through love, not with a crown of gold but with a crown of thorns.

The shepherds, the first to hear the good news, were not men of influence or power but ordinary workers tending their flocks in the fields. When the angel of the Lord appeared to them, announcing the birth of the Savior and declaring, "Ye shall find the babe wrapped in swaddling clothes, lying in a manger" (Luke 2:12), their hearts must have leaped with both awe and disbelief. A king in a manger? It defied all human expectations, yet it was a reflection of the very heart of God. The shepherds hurried to Bethlehem, and when they arrived, they found the scene just as the angel had said. There, in the stillness of the stable, they knelt before the manger, their hearts overwhelmed by the wonder of seeing the Savior of the world. Their joy and worship were a testament to the power of the manger's message: that God had come near, not to the mighty but to the meek, not to the proud but to the humble.

The wise men, too, were drawn to the child in the manger. Though they came later, guided by the star, their journey was one of faith and anticipation. They were men of learning and influence, yet when they arrived, they bowed before the child, offering gifts of gold, frankincense, and myrrh, recognizing Him as the true King, Priest, and Sacrifice. The contrast could not have been more profound: men of wealth and wisdom kneeling before a child in a manger, acknowledging the divine mystery of His birth. The manger, though simple and unassuming, had become a place of worship, a throne of humility that revealed the greatness of God's love.

The manger's message is one of profound humility and grace. It reminds us that Jesus did not come to seek power or privilege but to serve and to save. He was born in a stable, laid in a manger, and lived a life of humility so that He could meet us where we are. The manger declares that God's love knows no boundaries, that it reaches to the lowliest of places and the humblest of hearts. It is a call to come and see, to kneel in worship, and to marvel at the depth of His grace. Through the manger, we see a God who is not distant or detached but one who is near, who entered our world to bring us hope, peace, and salvation.

The manger also points us to the cross, for the humility of Christ's birth foreshadowed the humility of His death. The One who was laid in a wooden manger would one day be nailed to a wooden cross, giving His life as a ransom for many (Matthew 20:28). The manger, like the cross, is a symbol of God's love—a love that is sacrificial, selfless, and unconditional. It is a reminder that Jesus came not to be served but to serve, not to be exalted but to humble Himself, taking the form of a servant so that we might be lifted up (Philippians 2:5-8).

As we reflect on the manger, we are invited to embrace its message of humility and grace. It challenges us to lay aside our pride and to approach God with the same simplicity and faith as the shepherds and wise men. The manger calls us to recognize that true greatness is found not in power or position but in love and service. It invites us to make room in our hearts for the Savior, to allow Him to transform the ordinary places of our lives into sacred spaces where His presence dwells.

The manger, a throne of humility, continues to speak to us today. Its message is timeless, a reminder that the Savior who was born in Bethlehem is still Emmanuel, God with us. Through the manger, we see the heart of God, a heart that longs to dwell with His people, to bring light to their darkness, and to offer them the gift of eternal life. The manger invites us to come and behold the Lamb of God, who takes away the sin of the world (John 1:29), and to worship Him with all our hearts. It is a symbol of hope, a beacon of love, and a testament to the greatness of a God who chose to make His throne among us in the humblest of places. Through the manger, we are reminded that no place is too lowly, no heart too broken, for the presence of the Savior. It calls us to worship, to wonder, and to rejoice in the gift of Christ, the King who reigns from a throne of humility and whose love knows no bounds.

Day 13 - Bethlehem

Bethlehem, a small and seemingly insignificant town nestled in the hills of Judea, was chosen by God to be the birthplace of the Savior of the world, a place whose name would echo throughout eternity. Its name, meaning "House of Bread," carries a prophetic significance, for it was here that the Bread of Life would come to nourish a starving world (John 6:35). Bethlehem's history was rich with meaning, yet its humble reputation made it an unlikely setting for the greatest event in history. It was not a grand city like Jerusalem, nor a place of power like Rome, but a quiet, unassuming town whose simplicity reflected the humility of God's plan. The prophet Micah had foretold its importance centuries earlier, declaring, "But thou, Bethlehem Ephratah, though thou be little among the thousands of Judah, yet out of thee shall He come forth unto me that is to be ruler in Israel; whose goings forth have been from of old, from everlasting" (Micah 5:2). This prophecy, hidden in the pages of Scripture, revealed God's sovereign choice of Bethlehem as the stage for His greatest work of redemption.

Bethlehem's story began long before the night of Christ's birth. It was the home of Ruth and Boaz, whose love story laid the foundation for the lineage of David and ultimately for the Messiah. It was here that Ruth, a Moabitess, found redemption and a place among God's people, her life foreshadowing the inclusion of all nations in God's redemptive plan. From Bethlehem came David, the shepherd boy who became king, a man after God's own heart, and the one through whose lineage the eternal King would come. The fields surrounding Bethlehem were the very pastures where David tended his sheep, learning the heart of a shepherd, a heart that would reflect the Good Shepherd who was to come (John 10:11). Bethlehem, though small and humble, was chosen by God to play a pivotal role in His story, a reminder that He often uses the lowly and unexpected to accomplish His purposes.

On the night of Jesus' birth, Bethlehem was bustling with activity as people from all over Judea gathered to be counted for the census decreed by Caesar Augustus. Mary and Joseph, weary from their journey from Nazareth, arrived in the town seeking shelter, but there was no room for them in the inn. The streets were crowded, the inns were full, and the noise of the census drowned out any sense of quiet. Yet, in the midst of this chaos, God was orchestrating the fulfillment of His plan. Mary, heavy with child, was led to a stable, a place meant for animals, not kings, and it was here, in the humblest of settings, that she gave birth to Jesus, the Son of God. She wrapped Him in swaddling clothes and laid Him in a manger, a feeding trough that became a throne for the King of Kings (Luke 2:7). Bethlehem, the chosen place, became the birthplace of the Savior, and its fields and hills witnessed the arrival of the One who would change the course of history.

As the world slept, unaware of the miracle taking place, an angel of the Lord appeared to shepherds in the fields nearby, declaring, "Fear not: for, behold, I bring you good tidings of great joy, which shall be to all people. For unto you is born this day in the city of David a Saviour, which is Christ the Lord" (Luke 2:10-11). The angel's announcement was followed by a multitude of the heavenly host praising God and proclaiming, "Glory to God in the highest, and on earth peace, good will toward men" (Luke 2:14). The shepherds, men of humble means and simple lives, hurried to Bethlehem, their hearts filled with awe and wonder. They found Mary, Joseph, and the baby lying in a manger, just as the angel had said, and in that moment, they became the first witnesses to the fulfillment of God's promise. Bethlehem, the chosen place, was now the center of the greatest story ever told, its quiet hills forever marked by the footsteps of those who came to see the newborn King.

The wise men, following the star from the east, also made their way to Bethlehem. Their journey was one of faith and determination, for they recognized the significance of the star that led them to the place where the King of the Jews had been born. When they arrived, they presented their gifts of gold, frankincense, and myrrh, bowing in worship before the child who would bring salvation to the world (Matthew 2:11). Bethlehem, though small and seemingly unimportant, became a gathering place for shepherds and kings, for those who sought the Savior with humble hearts and those who brought treasures fit for a king. It was a place where the divine met the ordinary, where heaven touched earth, and where the light of God's glory shone in the darkness.

Bethlehem's significance is a reminder of God's ability to use the humble and overlooked for His glory. It was not the size or status of the town that mattered but God's sovereign choice to make it the birthplace of His Son. Bethlehem's story speaks of a God who values faithfulness over fame, humility over grandeur, and obedience over recognition. It challenges us to see that God's greatest works often begin in the most unexpected places and through the most unlikely people. Just as Bethlehem was chosen to cradle the Savior, so too can our own lives become places where God's presence dwells and His glory is revealed.

The story of Bethlehem calls us to reflect on the humility of Christ's birth and the depth of God's love. It invites us to come to the manger, to kneel in worship before the One who left the glory of heaven to be born in a stable, to walk among us, and to give His life for our redemption. Bethlehem reminds us that God's ways are higher than our ways (Isaiah 55:9) and that His plans, though often hidden from the world, are perfect and full of purpose. The town's role in the story of salvation is a testament to God's faithfulness, a reminder that His promises never fail and that His timing is always right.

As we think of Bethlehem, we are drawn to the truth that God is near, that He entered our world in the most humble of ways to bring us hope, peace, and salvation. The town's hills and fields, once ordinary and unremarkable, became the setting for the most extraordinary event in history. Bethlehem, the chosen place, stands as a symbol of God's grace, a place where His love was made manifest and His light began to shine in the darkness. It is a call to trust in His plans, to see His hand at work in the ordinary moments of our lives, and to rejoice in the gift of His Son, who came to save us and to bring us into His eternal kingdom. Through Bethlehem, we are reminded that no place is too small, no heart too humble, for the presence of the Savior. It is a beacon of hope, a declaration of God's love, and a testament to the glory of the One who was born there, the King of Kings and Lord of Lords.

Day 14 - The Innkeeper

The innkeeper of Bethlehem is an unnamed figure in the story of Christ's birth, a shadowed character whose decision has echoed through history. On the night when the Savior of the world entered humanity, this innkeeper stood at the threshold of an extraordinary moment but failed to see its significance. Bethlehem was bustling with activity, filled with travelers who had come to be counted for the census decreed by Caesar Augustus. The streets were crowded, the inns were full, and the noise of the town drowned out any sense of the sacred. In the midst of this chaos came Joseph and Mary, weary from their long journey from Nazareth. Mary, heavy with child, felt the pangs of labor drawing near, her steps faltering as she and Joseph sought shelter. They arrived at the inn, a place where travelers sought rest, but the innkeeper, seeing the fullness of his accommodations and the pressures of the busy night, turned them away. "No room," he must have said, perhaps with a tone of apology or frustration, but his words carried more weight than he could have imagined. He directed them elsewhere, and the Holy Family was left to find shelter in a stable, a place meant for animals, not for the King of Kings.

The innkeeper's rejection was not born of malice or cruelty but of distraction, busyness, and a failure to recognize the divine in the ordinary. To him, Joseph and Mary were just another pair of weary travelers among many, their needs no different from those of the countless others who had sought a place to stay that night. Yet, in turning them away, the innkeeper missed the greatest miracle of all time: the birth of the Savior, Emmanuel, God with us. The stable, with its rough wooden walls and earthy smells, became the birthplace of the Messiah, while the inn remained filled with people unaware of the holy event unfolding nearby. The innkeeper, preoccupied with his duties, failed to see that his humble inn could have been transformed into the stage for God's greatest act of love.

It is easy to imagine the scene that night—the flickering light of oil lamps casting shadows on the walls, the noise of travelers settling in for the night, the clatter of dishes and the sound of voices filling the air. The innkeeper, busy with his work, moving from room to room, ensuring that his guests were comfortable, likely felt the weight of responsibility pressing on him. He was a man caught up in the demands of the moment, unaware that eternity was stepping into time just beyond his doors. The cries of the newborn Savior would soon echo from the stable, carried on the night air, but the innkeeper would not hear them, his focus fixed on the tasks at hand. In his busyness, he missed the miracle that could have changed his life forever.

The innkeeper's story is not unique, for it reflects a pattern that has played out through history and continues today. How often do we, like the innkeeper, become so consumed with the demands of life, so preoccupied with our own concerns, that we fail to see the presence of God in our midst? The innkeeper had the opportunity to offer shelter to the Son of God, to play a role in the greatest story ever told, yet he missed it because he did not recognize the significance of the moment. His rejection of Mary and Joseph was not intentional but borne out of the pressures of the moment, a decision made without understanding. In this way, the innkeeper serves as a cautionary figure, reminding us to be watchful, to make room in our hearts and lives for the Savior, and to recognize the divine in the midst of the ordinary.

Though the innkeeper turned them away, God's plan was not thwarted. The stable, lowly and humble, became the birthplace of the King of Kings. The manger, a feeding trough for animals, became His first throne, and the shepherds, ordinary men tending their flocks, became the first witnesses of His glory. The rejection of the innkeeper did not diminish the significance of the moment but highlighted the humility of Christ's arrival. Jesus came not to seek comfort or grandeur but to meet humanity in its most humble and broken places. The stable, with all its simplicity, reflected the heart of His mission—a mission to save the lost, to bring light to the darkness, and to offer hope to the hopeless.

The innkeeper's story challenges us to examine our own lives. Are we, like him, so busy, so consumed with the demands of the world, that we fail to make room for Jesus? Do we turn Him away because we are too distracted to recognize His presence? The innkeeper missed the miracle because he saw only the surface, the outward appearance of a young couple in need, and failed to perceive the divine purpose unfolding before him. His story calls us to look beyond the noise and distractions of life, to open our eyes and hearts to the presence of God, and to make room for Him in every area of our lives.

Yet, there is grace even in the innkeeper's story. Though he missed the miracle that night, God's plan continued, and the Savior was born. This reminds us that even when we fail to see or make room for God, His purposes will still be accomplished. The innkeeper's missed opportunity serves as a call to be more attentive, to slow down, and to seek the presence of God in the midst of our busy lives. It is a reminder that the divine often comes in unexpected ways and places, and that we must be ready to receive Him, even when He appears in the humblest of forms.

The innkeeper's rejection of Mary and Joseph is a moment of great significance, not because it stopped God's plan but because it highlights the importance of making room for the Savior. It is a reminder that we, too, are faced with choices every day—choices to open our hearts and lives to Jesus or to turn Him away. The innkeeper missed the miracle, but we are given the opportunity to embrace it, to welcome the Savior into our hearts, and to allow His presence to transform our lives.

The innkeeper's story is not just about a man who turned away Mary and Joseph but about all of us and the choices we make. It is a call to slow down, to look beyond the busyness and distractions of life, and to see the presence of God in our midst. It is a reminder that even the smallest acts of kindness, the simplest gestures of hospitality, can become part of God's great story. Through the innkeeper, we are challenged to make room for Jesus, to welcome Him with open hearts, and to recognize the miracles unfolding around us every day. Let us not, like the innkeeper, miss the miracle but instead open the doors of our lives to the One who came to save us and bring us peace.

Day 15 - The Donkey

The donkey, a humble and unassuming creature, played a vital yet often overlooked role in the most sacred journey of all time—the journey to Bethlehem, where the Savior of the world would be born. Though the donkey had no voice to speak or name to remember, its silent service carried a profound message of humility, strength, and obedience. In a world where power and grandeur often overshadow quiet acts of faithfulness, the donkey stands as a symbol of how God uses the lowly and the ordinary to accomplish His extraordinary purposes. This creature, regarded as simple and insignificant by many, became a silent witness to the unfolding of God's greatest plan for humanity, bearing the weight of the woman chosen to carry the Son of God.

The journey to Bethlehem was not an easy one. Mary, heavy with child, sat upon the donkey's back as Joseph led the way through rugged terrain and long, dusty roads. The decree of Caesar Augustus had summoned them from their home in Nazareth to the town of their lineage, a journey of nearly 90 miles, made all the more arduous by Mary's condition. The donkey, sure-footed and steady, carried Mary with quiet endurance, its every step bringing them closer to the fulfillment of prophecy. The Scriptures do not tell us much about the animal, but its presence is inferred in the story of Mary and Joseph's travels. Without complaint or hesitation, the donkey bore its burden, a living example of humble service, embodying the patience and perseverance required for the sacred task.

As Mary sat upon the donkey, cradling within her the Savior of the world, the creature carried the weight of heaven's greatest gift. The rough paths and steep climbs were no obstacle to its unwavering faithfulness. It moved forward, step by step, its pace set by the gentle guidance of Joseph, who walked beside it, protecting Mary and the unborn child. The donkey's service was quiet but indispensable, a reminder that even the smallest acts of obedience can play a significant role in God's plan. Though unnoticed by the crowds and uncelebrated by history, the donkey's role was essential, demonstrating that God's work is often accomplished through the meek and lowly.

The donkey's presence in this sacred journey reflects the heart of God, who chooses the weak to confound the mighty and the foolish to shame the wise (1 Corinthians 1:27). This creature, so often associated with burdens and toil, became a vessel of divine purpose, carrying the mother of the Messiah to the place where the greatest miracle would occur. Its silence speaks volumes, reminding us that service does not need to be loud or recognized to be meaningful. The donkey's steady steps echo the quiet faithfulness that God calls His people to embody, a faithfulness that trusts in His plan even when the road is hard and the destination unclear.

When Mary and Joseph finally arrived in Bethlehem, the donkey stood among the humble surroundings of the stable, watching as Mary brought forth her firstborn son and laid Him in a manger (Luke 2:7). The stable, filled with the sounds of animals and the soft cries of the newborn Savior, became a place of holy wonder. The donkey, silent and steadfast, had fulfilled its role, bearing its burden with quiet dignity and faithfulness. Though it could not comprehend the significance of the moment, it had been a part of the journey that changed the world, a journey that brought the light of salvation into the darkness of humanity.

The story of the donkey does not end in Bethlehem. Its example continues to inspire, reminding us that God values humility and service over power and recognition. The donkey teaches us that no act of obedience is too small, no role too insignificant, to be used by God for His glory. It challenges us to embrace a spirit of humility, to serve faithfully in whatever tasks God places before us, and to trust that He can use even the simplest acts to accomplish His divine purposes. The donkey's journey with Mary and Joseph reminds us that God often works through the unnoticed and the overlooked, transforming ordinary moments into extraordinary milestones in His plan.

The donkey's story is a call to embrace the role of a servant, to walk humbly with God, and to carry out His will with quiet perseverance. Just as the donkey carried Mary to Bethlehem, we are called to bear the burdens of others, to serve with love and faithfulness, and to trust that God is at work in our lives even when our efforts seem small or insignificant. The donkey's silent witness to the birth of Christ challenges us to listen for the still, small voice of God and to follow His leading with unwavering trust.

The donkey's role in the journey to Bethlehem is a testament to the beauty of humble service. It reminds us that greatness in God's kingdom is not measured by recognition or applause but by faithfulness and obedience. The donkey carried the weight of the world's hope upon its back, a burden it bore without complaint, a task it fulfilled without seeking honor. In its simplicity, the donkey became a reflection of Christ Himself, who would later ride into Jerusalem on another donkey, a King who came not to be served but to serve and to give His life as a ransom for many (Matthew 21:5; Matthew 20:28).

As we reflect on the donkey's journey, we are reminded of our own calling to serve God with humility and faithfulness. The donkey, a silent servant in the journey, points us to the Savior it carried, the One who invites us to take His yoke upon us and learn from Him, for He is meek and lowly in heart (Matthew 11:29). The donkey's steps, though simple and unnoticed, led to the fulfillment of God's greatest promise, and its story encourages us to trust that our own acts of service, no matter how small, can be part of His greater plan.

The donkey's journey to Bethlehem is more than a footnote in the Christmas story; it is a profound reminder of the power of humility and the importance of faithfulness in the service of God. Its silent, steady steps carried the hope of the world, and its example challenges us to serve with the same quiet determination. Through the donkey, we see that God uses the lowly to accomplish His purposes, and we are reminded that our own journeys, though humble, can lead to the fulfillment of His promises. The donkey, a silent servant in the journey, calls us to walk with faith, to serve with humility, and to trust in the God who works through the ordinary to achieve the extraordinary.

Day 16 - Herod

Herod, known as Herod the Great, was a king consumed by power, paranoia, and an insatiable need to secure his throne at any cost. His reign was marked by grand building projects and political cunning, yet beneath the facade of strength and accomplishment lay a man driven by fear—a fear so deep that it would lead him to commit one of the most infamous atrocities in history. Herod's insecurities had long shaped his rule; he saw threats in every shadow, mistrusted even his own family, and eliminated anyone he perceived as a rival. This was the man who sat on the throne in Jerusalem when the wise men from the east arrived, bearing news that shook him to his core: "Where is He that is born King of the Jews? For we have seen His star in the east, and are come to worship Him" (Matthew 2:2). These words, spoken by strangers seeking a child, ignited a firestorm of fear and rage within Herod, for the very mention of a rival king was an affront to his fragile sense of security.

Herod, though a man of great political skill, was spiritually blind to the significance of the child the wise men sought. He did not see the star in the sky as a sign of God's promise or the fulfillment of prophecy but as a threat to his own power. His heart, hardened by years of self-interest and cruelty, could not comprehend the humility and love of the King who had been born in Bethlehem. Instead, Herod viewed this baby as a challenger to his throne, an adversary who must be eliminated at all costs. His fear was not rooted in righteousness or concern for his people but in the desperate clinging to earthly authority that he knew was fragile and fleeting.

Calling the chief priests and scribes, Herod demanded to know where Christ should be born. They answered, quoting the prophet Micah: "In Bethlehem of Judaea: for thus it is written by the prophet, And thou Bethlehem, in the land of Juda, art not the least among the princes of Juda: for out of thee shall come a Governor, that shall rule My people Israel" (Matthew 2:5-6). Herod, hearing these words, hatched a sinister plan. He summoned the wise men privately, feigning reverence and curiosity, and instructed them to find the child and bring him word so that he, too, might worship Him. But Herod's intentions were far from holy; his heart was set on destroying this newborn King, erasing the threat before it could take root. His words were a mask, a deceitful facade hiding his deadly resolve.

The wise men, unaware of Herod's true motives, departed on their journey, guided by the star that led them to the house where the child was. There, they fell down and worshiped Jesus, offering Him gifts of gold, frankincense, and myrrh (Matthew 2:11). But God, who sees the hearts of men and knows their plans, intervened. In a dream, He warned the wise men not to return to Herod, and they departed another way, leaving the king waiting and increasingly enraged. When Herod realized that the wise men had not returned, his fear boiled over into fury. He ordered a decree that would stain his legacy with blood: the massacre of all male children two years old and under in Bethlehem and the surrounding areas (Matthew 2:16). This horrifying act, known as the Slaughter of the Innocents, was Herod's desperate attempt to destroy the child he feared.

Herod's actions revealed the depths of his fear and the emptiness of his power. Though he sat on a throne and wielded authority, he was powerless against the will of God. The King he sought to destroy was no ordinary child but the Son of God, sent to bring salvation to the world. Herod's earthly power, built on manipulation and cruelty, was no match for the eternal kingdom of Christ, whose reign would be established not through force but through love and sacrifice. While Herod clung to his throne, terrified of losing it, Jesus, the true King, was cradled in His mother's arms, a picture of humility and grace.

Even in his rage, Herod could not thwart God's plan. An angel of the Lord appeared to Joseph in a dream, warning him to take the child and His mother and flee to Egypt. Obediently, Joseph rose by night and departed, ensuring the safety of the Savior (Matthew 2:13-14). Herod's decree, though devastating, could not reach the One whom God had sent to save the world. The child he feared was safe, protected by the very hand of God, and Herod's schemes ultimately crumbled under the weight of divine sovereignty.

Herod's life is a tragic example of what happens when fear and pride consume a person's heart. He had the opportunity to seek the Messiah, to bow before the true King, and to recognize the fulfillment of God's promises. Instead, he chose to resist, to cling to his earthly throne, and to fight against the very plan of God. His fear of a baby—a child born in a humble stable, surrounded by shepherds and animals—was rooted in his inability to see beyond himself. Herod's story reminds us that earthly power is fleeting and that those who fight against God's will only hasten their own downfall.

Herod's fear was not just of losing his throne but of losing control, of facing a power greater than his own. In his desperate attempt to preserve his rule, he revealed the emptiness of his authority and the fragility of his kingdom. His story stands in stark contrast to the true King he sought to destroy. While Herod ruled through fear, manipulation, and violence, Jesus came to rule through love, humility, and grace. While Herod clung to his throne with desperate hands, Jesus willingly laid aside His heavenly throne to walk among us, to serve, and to give His life as a ransom for many (Philippians 2:6-8).

The story of Herod, the king who feared a baby, is a cautionary tale for all who place their trust in power, wealth, or status. It challenges us to examine our own hearts and to ask whether we, like Herod, are resisting the reign of Christ in our lives. Are we clinging to our own thrones, unwilling to surrender control, or are we bowing before the true King, acknowledging His lordship and trusting in His plan? Herod's fear led him to reject the greatest gift ever given, but we are invited to receive it, to embrace the Savior who came to bring peace and salvation.

Herod's legacy is one of fear, pride, and missed opportunity, but his story points us to the eternal truth of God's sovereignty. No earthly king, no matter how powerful, can stand against the will of God. The baby Herod feared grew to be the Savior of the world, the King whose kingdom will never end (Luke 1:33). Herod's story reminds us that true power is not found in thrones or crowns but in the love and grace of Christ, who reigns forever and ever. Let us not, like Herod, resist the King, but instead, let us bow before Him, acknowledging Him as the Lord of our lives and the Savior of our souls.

Day 17 - Caesar Augustus

Caesar Augustus, the first emperor of Rome, ruled with a power and authority that stretched across the vast expanse of the known world. His name, Augustus, meaning "exalted one," reflected the grandeur and ambition of his reign, as he sought to establish peace and order through the might of the Roman Empire. To many, Augustus was the epitome of earthly power, a ruler who commanded armies, controlled wealth, and shaped the course of nations.

Yet, despite all his authority and grandeur, Caesar Augustus was an unwitting tool in the hands of the Almighty, a man whose decrees and ambitions served to fulfill a divine plan far greater than he could comprehend. While Augustus issued orders to solidify his rule and expand his legacy, God used his actions to bring about the fulfillment of ancient prophecy and to usher in the arrival of the true King, Jesus Christ.

The decree of Caesar Augustus, recorded in the opening verses of Luke's Gospel, was a simple yet profound moment in history. "And it came to pass in those days, that there went out a decree from Caesar Augustus, that all the world should be taxed" (Luke 2:1). This decree, a command for a census to be taken across the empire, seemed to be an administrative act, a way for Augustus to assert his control, assess his population, and ensure the flow of taxes that supported his vast kingdom. To the citizens of the empire, it was an inconvenience, a disruption of their lives as they were required to travel to their ancestral towns to be registered. Yet, beneath the surface of this worldly decree lay the hand of God, orchestrating events to bring about the fulfillment of His promises.

For Mary and Joseph, the decree of Caesar Augustus set in motion a journey that would forever change the world. Living in Nazareth, far from the town of Bethlehem, they were compelled to travel to the city of David, their ancestral home, to comply with the emperor's command. Mary, heavy with child, made the arduous journey alongside Joseph, her faith and trust in God carrying her through the difficulties of the road. The prophecy of Micah had foretold that the Messiah would be born in Bethlehem: "But thou, Bethlehem Ephratah, though thou be little among the thousands of Judah, yet out of thee shall He come forth unto me that is to be ruler in Israel; whose goings forth have been from of old, from everlasting" (Micah 5:2). Though Caesar Augustus issued the decree with no knowledge of this prophecy, his actions were the very means by which God ensured that His word would be fulfilled. The emperor, in all his power and pride, was unknowingly serving the will of the Most High, his decree becoming a key moment in the divine story of salvation.

As Mary and Joseph arrived in Bethlehem, the small town was bustling with activity, filled with travelers who had come to be counted for the census. In the midst of the chaos, the Savior of the world was born, not in a palace or a grand home, but in a humble stable, wrapped in swaddling clothes and laid in a manger (Luke 2:7). The child, Jesus, was the fulfillment of centuries of prophecy, the long-awaited Messiah who had come to bring light to the darkness and salvation to a fallen world. While Caesar Augustus sat on his throne in Rome, issuing decrees and reveling in his authority, the true King entered the world in quiet humility, His arrival announced not by imperial proclamation but by the angelic voices of the heavenly host declaring, "Glory to God in the highest, and on earth peace, good will toward men" (Luke 2:14).

The contrast between Caesar Augustus and Jesus Christ could not be more profound. Augustus ruled with power, using his authority to impose peace through force and control, while Jesus came to establish an eternal kingdom built on love, grace, and sacrifice. Augustus sought to expand his empire and secure his legacy through human means, yet his actions were used by God to further a plan that transcended earthly power and ambition. The decree that brought Mary and Joseph to Bethlehem was a reminder that God's sovereignty reigns supreme, that even the greatest rulers of the earth are subject to His will. "The king's heart is in the hand of the Lord, as the rivers of water: He turneth it whithersoever He will" (Proverbs 21:1). Augustus, in all his pride and power, was merely a vessel through which God's purposes were accomplished.

The legacy of Caesar Augustus, though grand in the eyes of the world, pales in comparison to the eternal impact of the child born in Bethlehem. Augustus built monuments, established laws, and brought a temporary peace known as the Pax Romana, but Jesus brought a peace that surpasses all understanding (Philippians 4:7), a peace that reconciles humanity to God and transforms hearts and lives. While Augustus's empire eventually crumbled, the kingdom of Christ continues to grow, its foundation unshakable and its reach eternal. The story of Augustus reminds us that God's plans are not hindered by human ambition or pride. In fact, He often works through the actions of those who do not even acknowledge Him, using their decisions to accomplish His will.

The story of Caesar Augustus also invites us to reflect on the nature of true power and authority. Augustus, who ruled the known world, was unaware that his decree would be remembered not for its political impact but for its role in fulfilling God's plan of redemption. His name, once exalted by men, now serves as a footnote in the story of the Savior who was born during his reign. This reminds us that earthly power is fleeting, that the works of human hands will one day fade, but the works of God endure forever. "The counsel of the Lord standeth for ever, the thoughts of His heart to all generations" (Psalm 33:11).

As we consider the role of Caesar Augustus in the story of Christ's birth, we are reminded of the sovereignty of God, who orchestrates all things for His glory and the good of His people. Augustus's decree, though issued for worldly reasons, became a key moment in the unfolding of God's eternal plan. His story challenges us to trust in God's providence, to believe that He is at work even in the midst of human decisions and events that may seem unrelated to His purposes. It calls us to see that no ruler, no empire, and no power on earth can stand against the will of the Almighty.

Caesar Augustus, the unwitting tool of prophecy, serves as a reminder that God's plans cannot be thwarted. His story is a testament to the truth that God's ways are higher than our ways and His thoughts than our thoughts (Isaiah 55:9). While Augustus sought to strengthen his rule, God used his actions to fulfill the promise of salvation, bringing forth the One who would reign forever as the King of Kings and Lord of Lords. Through Augustus, we see the power of God to work through all things, directing history toward the ultimate goal of His glory and the redemption of His people. Let us marvel at the wisdom and sovereignty of our God, who uses even the actions of earthly kings to bring about His eternal purposes, and let us bow in worship before the true King, Jesus Christ, whose kingdom will never end.

Day 18 - The Stable

The stable, a simple structure meant to shelter animals, became the most extraordinary place on earth the night Jesus was born. It was a place of rough wooden beams, dusty straw, and the earthy smell of livestock, a humble and unassuming shelter that seemed far removed from the majesty and glory of heaven. Yet, it was here, in this lowly setting, that the King of Kings and Lord of Lords entered the world, bringing with Him the light of salvation and the promise of redemption. The stable, though small and insignificant in the eyes of the world, was chosen by God to be the birthplace of His Son, a reflection of His heart for the humble, the meek, and the lowly. In its simplicity, the stable became a sacred space, the first glimpse of heaven on earth, where the divine met the ordinary and the eternal touched the temporal.

On that holy night, the stable stood silent and still, unaware of the miracle about to unfold within its walls. Mary and Joseph, weary from their journey to Bethlehem, found no room in the crowded inns, and so they turned to the stable, a place of refuge in their time of need. Mary, heavy with child, knew the time had come, and in the quiet of the night, surrounded by the animals and the soft glow of a lamp, she brought forth her firstborn son. She wrapped Him in swaddling clothes, simple strips of cloth, and laid Him in a manger, a feeding trough that became the first cradle of the Savior (Luke 2:7). In that moment, the stable was transformed into a holy sanctuary, its humble walls witnessing the greatest event in history—the incarnation of God in human form.

The stable, though modest and unadorned, was filled with the glory of heaven, for it cradled the One who is the image of the invisible God, the firstborn of every creature (Colossians 1:15). The cries of the newborn Savior pierced the stillness, a sound that carried the promise of hope and salvation to a weary world. The straw that lined the manger became a throne for the King of Kings, and the stable, with all its roughness and simplicity, reflected the humility of the One who came not to be served but to serve, and to give His life as a ransom for many (Matthew 20:28). The stable's lowly setting was no accident; it was a deliberate choice by God, a declaration that His kingdom is not of this world (John 18:36) and that His love reaches to the most humble and broken places.

The stable was not empty that night, for the animals that called it home became silent witnesses to the miracle of Christ's birth. The soft sounds of their breathing and the rustling of straw were the only accompaniment to the sacred moment. These creatures, unassuming and unaware, stood in the presence of their Creator, the One who spoke them into existence (Genesis 1:24-25). The stable's simplicity and quietness provided a contrast to the grandeur of heaven, yet it was in this humble place that the fullness of God's love was revealed. The One who was born there would later describe Himself as meek and lowly in heart (Matthew 11:29), and His birth in a stable foreshadowed the humility and sacrifice that would define His earthly ministry.

Outside the stable, the world carried on as usual, unaware of the miracle taking place within. Yet, heaven could not remain silent. An angel of the Lord appeared to shepherds in the fields nearby, announcing the good news: "Fear not: for, behold, I bring you good tidings of great joy, which shall be to all people. For unto you is born this day in the city of David a Saviour, which is Christ the Lord" (Luke 2:10-11). As the shepherds listened, a multitude of the heavenly host filled the sky, praising God and saying, "Glory to God in the highest, and on earth peace, good will toward men" (Luke 2:14). The stable, though simple and quiet, was the focal point of heaven's celebration, the place where God's plan of redemption began to unfold.

The shepherds, hastening to Bethlehem, arrived at the stable to see the newborn King. Their rough hands, accustomed to tending sheep, trembled as they knelt before the manger, their hearts overwhelmed by the sight of the Savior. They marveled at the simplicity of the setting, yet they recognized the holiness of the moment. The stable, though humble, had become a place of worship, its walls echoing with the prayers and praises of those who had been chosen to witness the miracle of Christ's birth. The shepherds, having seen the child, returned to their fields, glorifying and praising God for all they had heard and seen (Luke 2:20). The stable, Heaven's first glimpse, had changed their lives forever.

The stable's message is one of humility and grace. It reminds us that God chose to enter the world not in a palace or a temple but in a place of simplicity and need. The stable declares that God's love is not reserved for the powerful or the wealthy but is extended to all, especially the lowly and the humble. It is a call to come as we are, to kneel before the manger, and to receive the gift of salvation that was given freely and without condition. The stable challenges us to see that God often works through the ordinary and the unexpected, transforming the simplest of places into sacred spaces.

As we reflect on the stable, we are reminded of the humility of Christ, who left the glory of heaven to be born in a place meant for animals, who took on human flesh to walk among us, and who gave His life to redeem us. The stable, rough and unadorned, points us to the cross, where the humility of Christ's birth would be mirrored in the humility of His death. The wood of the manger foreshadowed the wood of the cross, and the simplicity of the stable reflected the sacrificial love that would define His mission. The stable, Heaven's first glimpse, is a symbol of God's willingness to meet us where we are, to enter our brokenness, and to bring us into His light.

The stable's story does not end with the birth of Christ, for its message continues to resonate through the ages. It reminds us that no place is too humble, no heart too broken, for the presence of the Savior. The stable calls us to embrace the simplicity of faith, to set aside the distractions and busyness of life, and to focus on the miracle of God's love made flesh. It invites us to see that the most profound moments of our lives often happen in the simplest of settings, and that God's presence can transform even the most ordinary places into holy ground.

The stable, Heaven's first glimpse, stands as a testament to the greatness of God's love and the humility of His plan. It is a place where the eternal met the temporal, where the infinite became finite, and where the glory of heaven shone in the darkness of earth. Through the stable, we see the heart of God, a heart that longs to dwell with His people and to bring them into His presence. The stable invites us to come and see, to kneel in worship, and to rejoice in the gift of the Savior who was born there. It is a reminder that God's love knows no boundaries and that His light can shine in even the humblest of places, offering hope, peace, and salvation to all who come to Him.

Day 19 - The Baby Jesus

The Baby Jesus, born on that holy night in Bethlehem, was more than just a child; He was the fulfillment of centuries of prophecy, the embodiment of God's love, and the Light that pierced the darkness of a weary and broken world. His birth was humble, taking place in a stable among animals, His first bed a manger lined with straw. Yet, in this simplicity lay the profound truth of God's plan: the Savior of the world had come, not as a conquering king clothed in splendor but as a helpless infant, fully divine yet fully human. The cries of the newborn Savior echoed in the stillness, a sound that carried the promise of hope, redemption, and eternal life. In that tiny form, wrapped in swaddling clothes, was the One who would change the course of history, the Word made flesh, dwelling among us (John 1:14). The Baby Jesus, though small and vulnerable, was the Light that would shine in the darkness, and the darkness would not overcome it (John 1:5).

The world into which Jesus was born was a world steeped in darkness. Rome ruled with an iron hand, and oppression, fear, and injustice were daily realities for many. The people of Israel had long awaited the Messiah, clinging to the promises of the prophets who foretold His coming. "For unto us a child is born, unto us a son is given: and the government shall be upon His shoulder: and His name shall be called Wonderful, Counsellor, The mighty God, The everlasting Father, The Prince of Peace" (Isaiah 9:6). Yet, when the time came, the arrival of the Messiah was not marked by royal proclamations or grand celebrations but by the quiet miracle of His birth in a stable. The Baby Jesus, the Light of the world, came into the darkness unnoticed by the powerful and celebrated by the humble—a reflection of the very heart of God.

Mary, His mother, held Him close, her heart overflowing with awe and wonder. She had been told by the angel Gabriel that this child would be called the Son of the Highest and that His kingdom would have no end (Luke 1:32-33). Now, as she gazed into the face of her newborn son, she marveled at the mystery of God's plan. The Baby Jesus, so small and fragile, was the Savior who had come to redeem His people, the Lamb of God who would take away the sin of the world (John 1:29). Mary pondered these things in her heart, treasuring the moment and the truth that her child was the Light sent to illuminate the path to God.

The first to hear the news of His birth were not rulers or priests but shepherds, men of lowly status who kept watch over their flocks by night. An angel of the Lord appeared to them, and the glory of the Lord shone around them, dispelling the darkness and filling their hearts with both fear and awe. "Fear not," the angel said, "for, behold, I bring you good tidings of great joy, which shall be to all people. For unto you is born this day in the city of David a Saviour, which is Christ the Lord" (Luke 2:10-11). The shepherds hurried to Bethlehem, their hearts filled with wonder, and when they found Mary, Joseph, and the Baby Jesus lying in the manger, they knelt in worship, recognizing that they were in the presence of the promised Messiah. The Light had come, and it shone brightly in that humble stable, illuminating the truth of God's love and faithfulness.

The wise men from the east, guided by a star, also came to worship Him. These men of wealth and learning traveled far, bringing gifts of gold, frankincense, and myrrh, each symbolizing a facet of the child's identity: gold for His kingship, frankincense for His divinity, and myrrh for His sacrifice. When they saw the Baby Jesus, they fell to their knees, acknowledging Him as the true King, the Light who had come to guide the nations. The star that led them to Him was a beacon of hope, a reminder that God's light shines even in the darkest of times, leading those who seek Him to the Savior.

The Baby Jesus, though born in obscurity, was the fulfillment of God's promise to bring salvation to the world. He came to dispel the darkness of sin and death, to reconcile humanity to God, and to offer eternal life to all who would believe in Him. "I am the light of the world," He would later declare. "He that followeth me shall not walk in darkness, but shall have the light of life" (John 8:12). His birth marked the beginning of a new chapter in the story of redemption, a chapter written in the light of God's grace and love. The Baby Jesus was the dawn of a new day, the Light that would never be extinguished, shining brightly in the hearts of those who receive Him.

The significance of the Baby Jesus extends far beyond the manger. His light continues to shine, offering hope to the hopeless, peace to the troubled, and joy to the sorrowful. He is the Light that guides us through the darkness of this world, illuminating the path of righteousness and leading us to the Father. His birth reminds us that God is near, that He has not abandoned us, and that His love is greater than any darkness we may face. The Baby Jesus is a testament to the truth that God's power is made perfect in weakness and that His light shines brightest in the most humble and unexpected places.

As we reflect on the Baby Jesus, we are reminded of the call to let His light shine through us. "Ye are the light of the world," Jesus said. "A city that is set on a hill cannot be hid" (Matthew 5:14). Just as the Baby Jesus brought light into the darkness, we are called to carry His light into a world in need, to share the good news of His love and salvation, and to reflect His grace in all that we do. His light is not meant to be hidden but to shine brightly, drawing others to the hope and joy found in Him.

The Baby Jesus, the Light in the darkness, is the greatest gift the world has ever known. His birth was the fulfillment of God's promise to bring salvation to His people, and His light continues to shine in the hearts of those who believe. Through Him, we find hope, peace, and the assurance of eternal life. The Baby Jesus is a reminder that no darkness is too great for the light of God's love, and no heart is too broken for His grace. He is the Light that guides us, the Savior who redeems us, and the King who reigns forever. Let us kneel before the manger, as the shepherds and wise men did, and worship the One who came to bring light into our darkness, the Baby Jesus, the Light of the world.

Day 20 - The Gifts of the Wise Men

The gifts of the wise men, gold, frankincense, and myrrh, were treasures both rich in value and deep in meaning, chosen with care to honor the child they believed to be the King of the Jews. These wise men, known as Magi, were scholars and seekers of truth, men who studied the stars and the mysteries of the heavens. They had traveled a great distance, guided by a star that led them to Bethlehem, to the house where the young child was. When they entered and saw Mary and the child, their hearts were filled with awe and reverence. Falling down in worship, they presented their gifts, offerings fit for a King. Each gift carried profound significance, not only reflecting the identity of the child but also pointing to His mission and the ultimate purpose of His coming. These treasures, given in faith and adoration, became symbols of the King, the High Priest, and the Savior who would change the world forever.

The first gift, gold, was a recognition of Jesus' royal status. Gold, a treasure of kings, symbolized wealth, power, and authority. By offering gold, the wise men acknowledged Jesus as the King of Kings, the promised ruler whose kingdom would have no end (Isaiah 9:7). This was no ordinary child; He was the fulfillment of the prophecy that a star would rise out of Jacob and a scepter out of Israel (Numbers 24:17). The gold laid at His feet reflected the glory and majesty of His reign, a reign not defined by earthly thrones or crowns but by the eternal authority of God. This gift, given in humility and devotion, declared that Jesus was the rightful King, not only of Israel but of all creation. Yet, the King they worshiped was unlike any other, for He came not to be served but to serve, to lead not by force but by love, and to establish a kingdom of peace and righteousness that would endure forever.

The second gift, frankincense, was an offering that spoke of Jesus' divinity and His role as the High Priest who would mediate between God and man. Frankincense, a fragrant resin used in temple worship, was burned as an offering to God, its sweet-smelling smoke rising as a symbol of prayer and worship. By presenting frankincense, the wise men proclaimed Jesus as more than a king; He was the Son of God, worthy of worship and adoration. This gift pointed to His role as the mediator of a new covenant, the one who would bridge the gap between a holy God and sinful humanity. As the aroma of frankincense filled the air, it symbolized the prayers of the faithful and the intercession of the Savior, who would one day offer Himself as the ultimate sacrifice. The gift of frankincense was a reminder that Jesus came to draw people into the presence of God, to bring reconciliation and restore the relationship that had been broken by sin.

The third gift, myrrh, carried a somber and prophetic significance, pointing to the sacrifice that Jesus would make for the salvation of the world. Myrrh, a spice used for anointing and embalming, was a symbol of suffering and death. While the other gifts celebrated His kingship and divinity, myrrh foreshadowed the cross, where Jesus would lay down His life as the Lamb of God who takes away the sin of the world (John 1:29). This gift was a stark reminder that the child in the manger was born to die, that His mission was not only to reign but to redeem. Myrrh spoke of the suffering He would endure, the wounds He would bear, and the victory He would achieve through His sacrifice. It pointed to the ultimate act of love, where Jesus would give His life as a ransom for many, conquering sin and death and opening the way to eternal life for all who believe.

These three gifts, gold, frankincense, and myrrh were not just material offerings but profound declarations of faith. The wise men, though they came from a distant land and a different culture, recognized in Jesus the fulfillment of divine prophecy. Their gifts reflected the depths of their understanding and the sincerity of their worship. Each gift revealed a truth about Jesus: His kingship, His divinity, and His sacrifice. The gold proclaimed Him as the King of Kings, the ruler whose kingdom would never fade. The frankincense declared Him as the High Priest, the one who would bring people into the presence of God. The myrrh foretold His death, the sacrifice that would bring salvation to the world. Together, these gifts told the story of who Jesus is and why He came, encapsulating the gospel message in their symbolism.

The journey of the wise men and their gifts remind us of the importance of seeking Jesus with our whole hearts and offering Him the best of what we have. Their gifts were costly, their journey long and challenging, but they came with joy and purpose, knowing that the one they sought was worth every sacrifice. Their actions challenge us to consider what we bring to Jesus. Do we offer Him our best, the treasures of our hearts, our worship, and our lives? Do we, like the wise men, kneel before Him in humility and reverence, acknowledging Him as our King, our Savior, and our God? Their gifts, though material, were given with hearts full of faith, and they remind us that true worship is not about the value of what we give but the spirit in which we give it.

The story of the wise men and their gifts also speaks to the universal nature of Jesus' mission. These men were Gentiles, outsiders to the covenant of Israel, yet they were among the first to recognize and worship the Messiah. Their journey and their offerings foreshadowed the inclusion of all nations in God's plan of salvation, the promise that the light of Christ would shine for all people. The gifts of the wise men remind us that Jesus is not just the King of the Jews but the Savior of the world, and they call us to share the good news of His love and grace with everyone.

As we reflect on the gifts of the wise men, we are reminded of the incredible gift that Jesus Himself is to us. He is the King who reigns in righteousness, the High Priest who intercedes for us, and the Savior who gave His life for our redemption. The wise men's gifts were treasures fit for a king, but they pale in comparison to the treasure we have in Jesus, the greatest gift of all. Their story inspires us to worship Him with all our hearts, to seek Him with all our strength, and to offer Him the best of who we are. The gifts of the wise men, given in faith and love, point us to the One who is worthy of all praise, the King who came to bring us into His eternal kingdom. Let us, like the wise men, lay our treasures at His feet and worship Him, for He is the King, the Priest, and the Savior who reigns forever and ever.

Day 21 - The Prophecies Fulfilled

The prophecies fulfilled in the birth, life, death, and resurrection of Jesus Christ stand as undeniable proof of God's faithfulness, a testament to His unchanging nature and the reliability of His Word. From the beginning of time, God wove His promises into the fabric of Scripture, revealing His redemptive plan through the prophets, each foretelling the coming of a Savior who would restore what was lost in the fall of man. These prophecies, spoken centuries before their fulfillment, painted a vivid picture of the Messiah, detailing His lineage, birthplace, mission, and ultimate sacrifice. Every prophecy, no matter how improbable it seemed at the time, was fulfilled with precision in the life of Jesus, proving that God's promises are sure, His timing is perfect, and His love for humanity is steadfast and eternal. The story of Jesus is the story of a faithful God who keeps His Word, whose plans cannot be thwarted, and whose purposes are always accomplished.

The prophecy of Jesus' birth in Bethlehem, spoken by the prophet Micah, is one of the clearest examples of God's sovereign orchestration of events. Micah declared, "But thou, Bethlehem Ephratah, though thou be little among the thousands of Judah, yet out of thee shall He come forth unto me that is to be ruler in Israel; whose goings forth have been from of old, from everlasting" (Micah 5:2). At the time of this prophecy, Bethlehem was a small and seemingly insignificant town, yet God chose it as the birthplace of the Savior. Centuries later, a decree from Caesar Augustus, calling for a census, compelled Mary and Joseph to journey to Bethlehem, fulfilling this ancient promise. Though they traveled under difficult circumstances, God's plan was at work, and Jesus was born in the very place foretold, a testament to His faithfulness and the unshakable truth of His Word.

The lineage of Jesus was also foretold with remarkable detail, confirming that He would come from the line of David. The prophet Isaiah spoke of a ruler who would arise from the house of Jesse, David's father, saying, "And there shall come forth a rod out of the stem of Jesse, and a Branch shall grow out of his roots" (Isaiah 11:1). This promise was reiterated throughout Scripture, highlighting the Davidic covenant and God's assurance that David's throne would be established forever. In the genealogies recorded in Matthew and

Luke, we see the fulfillment of this promise, tracing Jesus' lineage through David's line and proving that He is the rightful heir to the throne of Israel. God's faithfulness in preserving this lineage, despite the turmoil and challenges faced by Israel, underscores His sovereignty and His commitment to keeping His promises.

The manner of Jesus' birth was also foretold by the prophet Isaiah, who proclaimed, "Therefore the Lord Himself shall give you a sign; Behold, a virgin shall conceive, and bear a son, and shall call His name Immanuel" (Isaiah 7:14). This miraculous event, humanly impossible, was fulfilled in Mary, a young virgin chosen by God to bear His Son. When the angel Gabriel appeared to her, announcing that she would conceive by the Holy Ghost, Mary responded with faith and submission, saying, "Behold the handmaid of the Lord; be it unto me according to thy word" (Luke 1:38). The virgin birth of Jesus was a sign of God's power and faithfulness, a reminder that nothing is impossible with Him (Luke 1:37).

The prophecies concerning Jesus' mission and ministry were equally remarkable, revealing His role as the Savior and Redeemer of humanity. Isaiah described the Messiah as the one anointed to bring good news to the poor, to bind up the brokenhearted, and to proclaim liberty to the captives (Isaiah 61:1). Jesus Himself declared the fulfillment of this prophecy when He read these words in the synagogue in Nazareth, saying, "This day is this scripture fulfilled in your ears" (Luke 4:21). Throughout His ministry, Jesus fulfilled these promises, healing the sick, forgiving sins, and offering hope to the marginalized and downtrodden. His actions and words were the living proof of God's faithfulness, demonstrating that He came not to condemn the world but to save it (John 3:17).

Even the manner of Jesus' death was foretold with stunning accuracy, centuries before crucifixion was practiced as a form of execution. The psalmist David described the suffering of the Messiah, writing, "They pierced my hands and my feet" (Psalm 22:16), and Isaiah foretold the suffering servant who would bear the iniquities of many, saying, "He was wounded for our transgressions, He was bruised for our iniquities: the chastisement of our peace was upon Him; and with His stripes we are healed" (Isaiah 53:5). These prophecies were fulfilled in the crucifixion of Jesus, who willingly laid down His life as the ultimate sacrifice for sin. His death on the cross, though marked by unimaginable pain and suffering, was the fulfillment of God's promise to provide a way of salvation, a demonstration of His unchanging love and faithfulness.

The resurrection of Jesus, the cornerstone of the Christian faith, was also foretold in Scripture. David wrote, "For Thou wilt not leave my soul in hell; neither wilt Thou suffer Thine Holy One to see corruption" (Psalm 16:10). This prophecy found its fulfillment three days after Jesus' crucifixion, when He rose from the dead, conquering sin and death and proving His divinity. The resurrection stands as the ultimate proof of God's faithfulness, a reminder that His promises are not bound by time or circumstance. Through the resurrection, God demonstrated His power to bring life from death and to fulfill His word in ways that surpass human understanding.

The fulfillment of these prophecies is not just a historical record but a living testimony to the faithfulness of God. Each promise kept is a reminder that God's Word is true, that His plans are perfect, and that His love for us is unwavering. The prophecies concerning Jesus reveal the depth of God's commitment to redeeming His creation, His patience in carrying out His plan, and His ability to work all things together for good. They remind us that God's timing is not our timing, but His timing is always right. "The Lord is not slack concerning His promise, as some men count slackness; but is longsuffering to us-ward, not willing that any should perish, but that all should come to repentance" (2 Peter 3:9).

As we reflect on the fulfilled prophecies of Jesus, we are called to trust in God's promises for our own lives. The same God who faithfully brought forth the Savior will be faithful to complete the work He has begun in us (Philippians 1:6). The fulfilled prophecies of Scripture give us confidence that God's Word is true, that His plans are good, and that His promises are worth waiting for. They encourage us to hold fast to our faith, even in the face of doubt or difficulty, knowing that the God who kept His promises to Israel will keep His promises to us.

The prophecies fulfilled in Jesus also call us to worship and gratitude. They remind us of the extraordinary lengths God has gone to in order to save us, the meticulous detail of His plan, and the infinite love that motivated it. Each fulfilled prophecy is a declaration of His faithfulness, a testament to His sovereignty, and an invitation to trust Him with our lives. They call us to bow before the King who was promised, to embrace the Savior who was foretold, and to live in the light of His love and grace.

The story of fulfilled prophecy is the story of a faithful God who keeps His Word, whose plans are perfect, and whose love for us is unending. It is a story that invites us to trust Him, to worship Him, and to find our hope and confidence in Him. Through the prophecies fulfilled in Jesus, we see the faithfulness of a God who never fails, whose promises are sure, and whose love endures forever. Let us hold fast to His Word, for it is the unshakable foundation of our faith and the proof of His faithfulness, now and always.

Day 22 - The Journey to Bethlehem

THE JOURNEY TO BETHLEHEM, undertaken by Mary and Joseph, was far more than a physical trek across rugged terrain; it was a profound act of faith, a demonstration of their trust in God's path, even when the way was uncertain and the destination unknown. It was a journey prompted by the decree of Caesar Augustus, an earthly ruler who called for a census that required every man to return to his ancestral town. For Joseph, this meant leading his espoused wife, Mary, from Nazareth to Bethlehem, a journey of nearly 90 miles over rocky roads and hilly countryside. Mary, heavy with child, carried within her the Savior of the world, the fulfillment of centuries of prophecy and the hope of all humanity. Yet this divine purpose did not shield them from the challenges of the journey. They faced the discomfort of travel, the exhaustion of the road, and the uncertainty of what awaited them in Bethlehem. But through it all, their faith remained steadfast, their steps guided by a deep trust in the God who had called them to this moment.

From the moment the angel Gabriel appeared to Mary, announcing that she would conceive by the Holy Ghost and bear the Son of God, her life had been marked by a willingness to follow God's will, no matter the cost. Gabriel's words, "Fear not, Mary: for thou hast found favour with God" (Luke 1:30), must have resonated in her heart as she embarked on this arduous journey. She had responded to the angel's message with humility and faith, saying, "Behold the handmaid of the Lord; be it unto me according to thy word" (Luke 1:38).

Now, as she sat upon the back of a donkey, each step bringing her closer to Bethlehem, she must have reflected on the mystery and majesty of her calling. Beside her walked Joseph, a man of righteousness and quiet strength, who had also received a message from an angel, instructing him to take Mary as his wife despite the extraordinary circumstances of her pregnancy. Joseph's obedience and faith were evident as he led Mary along the winding paths, protecting her and trusting in the divine plan that was unfolding, even if it was beyond his understanding.

The road to Bethlehem was filled with challenges, yet it was also filled with the presence of God. Each step they took was part of a divine plan, orchestrated long before the foundations of the world were laid. The prophet Micah had foretold the significance of Bethlehem, saying, "But thou, Bethlehem Ephratah, though thou be little among the thousands of Judah, yet out of thee shall He come forth unto me that is to be ruler in Israel; whose goings forth have been from of old, from everlasting" (Micah 5:2). Mary and Joseph may not have fully understood the weight of this prophecy, but their obedience placed them in the center of God's redemptive plan. As they journeyed through valleys and over hills, they were fulfilling the words spoken by the prophets, their steps guided by the unseen hand of the Almighty. Each mile brought them closer to the moment when the Word would become flesh and dwell among us (John 1:14).

The physical demands of the journey were undeniable. The rough paths, the dusty air, and the long days of travel would have tested their endurance. Mary, nearing the time of her delivery, must have experienced discomfort and fatigue, yet her faith carried her forward. She bore within her the Light of the world, the One who would bring salvation to all people, and this knowledge gave her strength. Joseph, too, must have felt the weight of responsibility as he cared for Mary and ensured her safety. His quiet determination and steadfast faith reflected his trust in God's provision, even when the way was difficult. Together, they pressed on, trusting that God would provide for their needs and fulfill His promises.

When they finally arrived in Bethlehem, the town was crowded with travelers who had come for the census. The noise and chaos of the bustling streets must have been overwhelming, yet Mary and Joseph continued to trust in God's plan. They sought shelter, but there was no room for them in the inn. This rejection could have been a moment of despair, but instead, they found refuge in a stable, a place of simplicity and humility. It was here, in the quiet of the night, surrounded by animals and the soft glow of a lamp, that Mary gave birth to her firstborn son. She wrapped Him in swaddling clothes and laid Him in a manger, a feeding trough that became the first throne of the King of Kings (Luke 2:7). The stable, though humble and unassuming, was transformed into a place of holiness and wonder, for it was here that the Savior entered the world.

The journey to Bethlehem teaches us profound lessons about trusting God's path. It shows us that faith often requires us to step into the unknown, to walk difficult roads, and to endure challenges with the assurance that God is with us. Mary and Joseph's obedience and perseverance remind us that God's plans are higher than our plans and that His ways are perfect, even when they lead us through valleys and over rough terrain (Isaiah 55:8-9). Their journey calls us to trust in God's timing, to believe in His promises, and to follow His leading, even when the way is unclear.

This journey also reminds us that God is present in every step of our lives. Just as He guided Mary and Joseph to Bethlehem, fulfilling His purposes through their faithfulness, He walks with us on our journeys, offering His strength, peace, and guidance. The road may be long, and the destination may seem far away, but we can trust that God is at work, using every moment to bring about His good and perfect will (Romans 8:28). Mary and Joseph's journey to Bethlehem is a testament to God's sovereignty and faithfulness, a reminder that He is in control, even when the path is difficult.

As we reflect on the journey to Bethlehem, we are reminded of the beauty of trusting God's path. It calls us to surrender our fears, doubts, and uncertainties to Him, to walk by faith and not by sight (2 Corinthians 5:7), and to believe that He is working all things together for good. Mary and Joseph's journey encourages us to remain steadfast in our faith, to persevere through challenges, and to trust that God's promises will be fulfilled in His perfect timing. Their story is a powerful example of what it means to follow God's leading, even when the way is hard, and to trust that He will provide everything we need along the way.

The journey to Bethlehem was not just a physical journey; it was a journey of faith, hope, and trust in God's plan. It was a journey that led to the fulfillment of prophecy, the birth of the Savior, and the redemption of humanity. Mary and Joseph's willingness to follow God's path, no matter the cost, is an inspiration to us all, reminding us that God's ways are always good and that His plans for us are far greater than we can imagine. Let us, like Mary and Joseph, trust in God's path, walking forward in faith and confidence, knowing that He is with us every step of the way.

Day 23 - The Virgin Birth

The virgin birth of Jesus Christ stands as one of the greatest miracles in all of history, a profound and divine act of God that demonstrated His power, fulfilled His promises, and revealed the purity of His plan to bring salvation to the world. It was a miracle of purity and power, a moment when heaven touched earth, and the impossible became reality. The prophet Isaiah had foretold this miraculous event centuries before, declaring, "Therefore the Lord Himself shall give you a sign; Behold, a virgin shall conceive, and bear a son, and shall call His name Immanuel" (Isaiah 7:14). This prophecy, spoken in a time of uncertainty and fear, pointed to a Savior who would be both God and man, a Redeemer who would come not through human effort but through the divine intervention of the Almighty. The virgin birth was not just a sign; it was the foundation of the gospel, the assurance that Jesus Christ was indeed the Son of God, sent to save His people from their sins.

Mary, a young woman from the humble town of Nazareth, was chosen by God to be the vessel through which this miracle would come to pass. Her life was marked by simplicity and faith, qualities that prepared her for the extraordinary calling she would receive. When the angel Gabriel appeared to her, his greeting must have filled her with both awe and wonder: "Hail, thou that art highly favoured, the Lord is with thee: blessed art thou among women" (Luke 1:28). Mary, though troubled by the angel's words, listened as Gabriel revealed the divine plan: she would conceive and bring forth a son, and His name would be Jesus. "He shall be great, and shall be called the Son of the Highest: and the Lord God shall give unto Him the throne of His father David: And He shall reign over the house of Jacob for ever; and of His kingdom there shall be no end" (Luke 1:32-33). These words carried the weight of prophecy and promise, yet Mary, in her humility, asked a simple and practical question: "How shall this be, seeing I know not a man?" (Luke 1:34).

Gabriel's response revealed the divine nature of the miracle: "The Holy Ghost shall come upon thee, and the power of the Highest shall overshadow thee: therefore also that holy thing which shall be born of thee shall be called the Son of God" (Luke 1:35). In this moment, the miracle of the virgin birth was set in motion, a work of God that bypassed human limitations and displayed His infinite power. The Holy Ghost, the creative force of God, would overshadow Mary, and she would conceive the Savior without the involvement of a human father. This act of divine power ensured that Jesus would be born without the stain of sin, fully human yet fully divine, the perfect Lamb of God who would take away the sin of the world (John 1:29). Mary's response to this incredible revelation was a testament to her faith and obedience: "Behold the handmaid of the Lord; be it unto me according to thy word" (Luke 1:38). With these words, Mary surrendered to God's will, trusting in His plan and embracing the miracle that would forever change her life and the world.

The virgin birth was a miracle of purity, a reflection of God's holiness and His plan to bring a Savior into the world unstained by sin. Through this miraculous event, Jesus was born as the sinless Son of God, the only one capable of bridging the gap between a holy God and sinful humanity. His conception by the Holy Ghost ensured that He was free from the inherited sin nature of Adam, making Him the perfect sacrifice for the redemption of mankind. "For we have not an high priest which cannot be touched with the feeling of our infirmities; but was in all points tempted like as we are, yet without sin" (Hebrews 4:15). The purity of the virgin birth is a reminder of the holiness of God and the lengths to which He would go to save His people, sending His Son into the world through a miraculous and undefiled means.

At the same time, the virgin birth was a miracle of power, demonstrating God's ability to accomplish the impossible. Mary's conception was not the result of human effort or natural processes but of God's sovereign will and divine power. It was a reminder that nothing is too hard for the Lord (Jeremiah 32:17), a declaration of His authority over creation and His ability to fulfill His promises. The angel Gabriel affirmed this truth when he said to Mary, "For with God nothing shall be impossible" (Luke 1:37). The virgin birth was a moment when the power of God was made manifest, breaking into the natural world and revealing His glory in a way that could not be denied. It was a testament to His sovereignty and His commitment to His plan of redemption, a miracle that pointed to the truth that salvation is the work of God alone.

The virgin birth also fulfilled God's promises and confirmed the reliability of His Word. Throughout the Old Testament, God had spoken through the prophets, revealing His plan to send a Messiah who would redeem His people. From the promise in Genesis 3:15, where God declared that the seed of the woman would crush the serpent's head, to the prophecy in Isaiah 9:6, which described a child born to bring peace and establish an everlasting kingdom, the Scriptures pointed to the coming of Christ. The virgin birth fulfilled these promises with precision, demonstrating that God's Word is true and His plans are unshakable. "For all the promises of God in Him are yea, and in Him Amen, unto the glory of God by us" (2 Corinthians 1:20).

The miracle of the virgin birth also reveals the humility of God's plan. Jesus, the King of Kings and Lord of Lords, was not born in a palace or surrounded by wealth and grandeur but in a stable, wrapped in swaddling clothes and laid in a manger (Luke 2:7). His humble beginnings reflected the heart of God, who came not to be served but to serve, and to give His life as a ransom for many (Matthew 20:28). The virgin birth, taking place in the quiet and simplicity of Bethlehem, demonstrated that God's ways are not our ways and that His power is made perfect in weakness (2 Corinthians 12:9). It was a miracle that turned human expectations upside down, showing that God's plan for salvation would come not through force or power but through love, grace, and sacrifice.

As we reflect on the virgin birth, we are reminded of the depth of God's love for us. He sent His Son into the world through a miraculous means, fulfilling His promises and providing a way for us to be reconciled to Him. The virgin birth is a call to faith, a reminder that God is able to do exceedingly abundantly above all that we ask or think (Ephesians 3:20), and that His plans for us are good and perfect. It challenges us to trust in His power, to believe in His promises, and to surrender to His will, just as Mary did when she said, "Be it unto me according to thy word."

The virgin birth is a cornerstone of the Christian faith, a miracle that confirms the identity of Jesus as the Son of God and the Savior of the world. It is a testimony to the purity, power, and faithfulness of God, a reminder that He is able to accomplish His purposes in ways that surpass human understanding. Through the virgin birth, we see the heart of a God who loves us so deeply that He would send His Son to dwell among us, to live a sinless life, and to offer Himself as the perfect sacrifice for our sins. It is a miracle that invites us to worship, to marvel at the greatness of God, and to place our faith in the One who was born to save us. Let us celebrate the virgin birth as a miracle of purity and power, a divine act of love that brought light into the darkness and life to a world in need of redemption.

Day 24 - The Carpenter's Role

Joseph, the carpenter of Nazareth, was a man whose life was transformed by an extraordinary calling, and his role in the story of Jesus is one of strength, humility, and obedience. Though he is often a quiet figure in the narrative of Christ's birth, his actions speak volumes about his character and faith. Joseph was a simple man, a craftsman who worked with his hands to shape wood and build structures, providing for himself and those under his care. His life, before the angel of the Lord appeared to him, likely followed a steady rhythm of work, worship, and devotion to the traditions of his people. Yet, when the divine plan unfolded, Joseph's life took a turn that would test his faith and reveal his strength in obedience to God. His role as the earthly father of Jesus and the protector of Mary was not chosen by accident but ordained by the hand of God, who saw in Joseph a man of integrity, a man whose quiet strength and unwavering trust would serve as a foundation for the Holy Family.

Joseph's strength was first tested when he learned that Mary, his betrothed, was with child. Betrothal in Jewish custom was a binding agreement, and to discover that Mary was pregnant before they came together would have been a shattering revelation. As a righteous man, Joseph loved Mary but was also bound by the law, which could have led to public disgrace or even severe punishment for her. Yet, his love and compassion guided his decision to put her away quietly, sparing her from shame (Matthew 1:19). This choice alone revealed the depth of his character—his kindness, his restraint, and his desire to act with grace, even in the face of what he perceived as betrayal. But God had a greater plan for Joseph, a plan that required him to set aside his own understanding and trust completely in the divine purpose.

As Joseph wrestled with this decision, an angel of the Lord appeared to him in a dream, bringing a message that would change everything: "Joseph, thou son of David, fear not to take unto thee Mary thy wife: for that which is conceived in her is of the Holy Ghost. And she shall bring forth a son, and thou shalt call His name JESUS: for He shall save His people from their sins" (Matthew 1:20-21). These words must have filled Joseph with awe and reverence, yet they also demanded an extraordinary level of faith. To accept this message meant embracing a mystery beyond human understanding, taking on the responsibility of raising a child who was the Son of God, and standing beside Mary as she carried the Savior of the world. Joseph did not hesitate; when he awoke, he obeyed the command of the angel, taking Mary as his wife and stepping into the role God had prepared for him. His obedience was immediate and complete, reflecting a heart that trusted in God's plan, even when it defied reason.

Joseph's role as the earthly father of Jesus required him to protect and provide for his family in the face of great challenges. When the time came for the census decreed by Caesar Augustus, Joseph led Mary on the arduous journey to Bethlehem, where Jesus would be born. This journey, nearly 90 miles over rough terrain, was no small task, especially with Mary in the final stages of pregnancy. Yet Joseph carried the weight of responsibility with quiet strength, ensuring Mary's safety and guiding her to the place where prophecy would be fulfilled. Upon their arrival, finding no room in the inn, Joseph sought shelter in a stable, a humble and unexpected place that became the birthplace of the Savior. In this moment, Joseph's role as protector and provider was evident, as he created a space of warmth and safety for Mary to bring forth her firstborn son, wrapping Him in swaddling clothes and laying Him in a manger (Luke 2:7).

Joseph's strength in obedience continued to shine as he responded to the divine warnings and guidance given to him. After the wise men departed, an angel of the Lord appeared to Joseph in a dream, instructing him to flee to Egypt to protect the child from Herod's wrath: "Arise, and take the young child and His mother, and flee into Egypt, and be thou there until I bring thee word: for Herod will seek the young child to destroy Him" (Matthew 2:13). Without hesitation, Joseph rose in the night, gathered Mary and Jesus, and embarked on the journey to Egypt, trusting in God's provision and protection. This act of obedience, undertaken in the face of danger and uncertainty, demonstrated Joseph's unwavering faith and his commitment to his role as the protector of the Messiah.

In Egypt, Joseph once again displayed his strength and resourcefulness, providing for his family in a foreign land until it was safe to return. When the angel appeared to him again, instructing him to return to Israel, Joseph obeyed, settling in the town of Nazareth to raise Jesus in safety. His life as a carpenter, working diligently to provide for his family, was marked by humility and faithfulness. Though he lived in the background of the gospel narrative, his influence on Jesus' early years was profound. Joseph's example of integrity, hard work, and trust in God would have shaped the human upbringing of Jesus, instilling values and principles that reflected the character of the heavenly Father.

Joseph's role in the story of Jesus is a testament to the power of obedience and the strength that comes from trusting in God's plan. Though he was not a man of wealth or prominence, he was chosen by God because of his heart—a heart that was willing to follow, to serve, and to sacrifice for the sake of the divine purpose. His life reminds us that true strength is found not in power or position but in humility and faith. Joseph's quiet obedience, his willingness to set aside his own plans and embrace God's will, is an example for us all. He teaches us that God often calls us to tasks that require faith and courage, and that His strength is made perfect in our weakness (2 Corinthians 12:9).

The carpenter's role was one of selfless service, a reflection of the very mission of the child he raised. Just as Joseph protected and provided for Jesus, so Jesus would grow to be the protector and provider for all humanity, laying down His life as the ultimate act of love and obedience to the Father's will. Joseph's life points us to the greater story of redemption, reminding us that every act of obedience, no matter how small, plays a part in God's greater plan. His strength in obedience is an invitation to trust in God's path, to follow His leading, and to embrace the role He has prepared for us, knowing that He is faithful to guide and sustain us.

Joseph, the carpenter, may not have spoken many words in Scripture, but his life was a living testimony to the power of faith and obedience. His strength lay not in his own abilities but in his trust in God, his willingness to follow, and his unwavering commitment to the calling he had received. Through Joseph, we see the beauty of a life surrendered to God, a life that reflects the strength found in saying, "Be it unto me according to thy word." His story is a reminder that God uses ordinary people to accomplish extraordinary things, and that obedience, even in the face of uncertainty, is the key to fulfilling His divine purpose. Let us, like Joseph, walk in faith, trusting in God's strength and following His call with a heart of obedience, knowing that He is with us every step of the way.

Day 25 - The Angelic Song

The angelic song on the night of Jesus' birth was a moment when heaven's glory burst forth upon the earth, a divine proclamation that resounded through the stillness of the night, declaring the wonder of God's love and the joy of His salvation. In a quiet field outside Bethlehem, shepherds kept watch over their flocks, unaware that they were about to witness an event that would change the course of history. The night was ordinary, their tasks routine, until suddenly, the sky was filled with the brilliance of heaven's light, and an angel of the Lord appeared before them. The shepherds, overwhelmed with fear, trembled at the sight, for they were in the presence of the holy. Yet the angel's first words were words of comfort and assurance: "Fear not: for, behold, I bring you good tidings of great joy, which shall be to all people. For unto you is born this day in the city of David a Saviour, which is Christ the Lord" (Luke 2:10-11). These words, simple yet profound, carried the message of hope that the world had been waiting for—the Messiah had come, and His arrival was good news for all humanity.

As the angel continued, the shepherds listened with awe, their hearts beginning to grasp the significance of this moment. The angel spoke of a sign, a child wrapped in swaddling clothes and lying in a manger, a humble yet holy image that reflected the heart of God's plan. Then, as if the heavens could no longer contain their joy, a multitude of the heavenly host appeared, filling the sky with their radiant presence and lifting their voices in a song of praise: "Glory to God in the highest, and on earth peace, good will toward men" (Luke 2:14). This angelic song was not just a melody; it was a declaration, a celebration, and a revelation of the divine purpose. It proclaimed the glory of God, the peace that Jesus would bring, and the goodwill of God toward humanity, a message that resonated across the ages and continues to inspire hearts today.

"Glory to God in the highest"—these words were the opening notes of the heavenly chorus, a call to lift the name of God above all else, to recognize His majesty, and to give Him the honor He alone deserves. The angels, who had witnessed the splendor of creation and the sorrow of the fall, now rejoiced in the fulfillment of God's redemptive plan. The birth of Jesus was the ultimate demonstration of God's glory, His power, and His love, and the angels could not contain their praise. They exalted the Creator who had become a part of His creation, the King who had chosen to dwell among His people, and the Savior who had come to rescue the lost. The song of the angels was a reflection of the unceasing worship that fills the courts of heaven, a reminder that all of creation exists to glorify God and to declare His greatness.

"And on earth peace"—this phrase spoke of the peace that Jesus would bring, a peace that transcends human understanding and reaches into the deepest corners of the human heart. The angels proclaimed the arrival of the Prince of Peace, the One who would reconcile humanity to God and bring an end to the enmity caused by sin. This peace was not merely the absence of conflict but the presence of wholeness, healing, and restoration. It was a peace that offered hope to the broken, comfort to the weary, and salvation to the lost. The angels' song declared that through Jesus, the peace of heaven had come to earth, a peace that would endure forever and transform the lives of all who received it.

"Good will toward men"—these words revealed the heart of God, His love and kindness extended to all people. The birth of Jesus was the ultimate expression of God's goodwill, His desire to save and redeem His creation. The angels' song declared that this goodwill was not limited to a select few but was a gift for all who would believe. It was a message of inclusion, a reminder that God's love knows no boundaries and that His salvation is available to every nation, tribe, and tongue. The goodwill of God, displayed in the gift of His Son, was a call to all humanity to come and see, to kneel before the Savior, and to receive the grace that only He can give.

The angelic song, though brief, carried a depth of meaning that cannot be fully grasped. It was a moment when heaven and earth met, when the divine plan was unveiled, and when the glory of God shone in the darkness. The shepherds, though humble and unassuming, were chosen to witness this extraordinary event, a reflection of God's heart for the lowly and the marginalized. Their response to the angelic song was one of faith and action. They said to one another, "Let us now go even unto Bethlehem, and see this thing which is come to pass, which the Lord hath made known unto us" (Luke 2:15). With haste, they left their flocks and made their way to the stable, where they found Mary, Joseph, and the baby lying in a manger, just as the angel had said. As they gazed upon the Savior, their hearts were filled with wonder, and they glorified and praised God for all they had heard and seen (Luke 2:20).

The angelic song continues to resonate through the ages, its message as relevant today as it was on the night of Jesus' birth. It is a call to lift our eyes to heaven, to glorify God for His incredible gift, and to embrace the peace and goodwill that He offers through His Son. It challenges us to join the chorus of praise, to declare the glory of God in our own lives, and to share the good news of His love with others. The song of the angels is a reminder that the birth of Jesus is not just a historical event but a living reality, a gift that brings light to our darkness and hope to our hearts.

As we reflect on the angelic song, we are invited to experience the wonder and joy of that holy night, to join in the worship of the heavenly host, and to proclaim the glory of God in the highest. Let us, like the shepherds, respond with faith and action, seeking the Savior and sharing the good tidings of great joy with all who will listen. The angelic song is a timeless anthem of praise, a declaration of God's love, and a reminder that through Jesus, peace and goodwill have come to earth. Let us lift our voices in harmony with the angels, giving glory to God and rejoicing in the gift of His Son, the Savior of the world.

Day 26 - The Shepherds' Faith

The shepherds' faith, displayed on the night of Jesus' birth, is one of the most profound and heart-stirring examples of trust and obedience found in the Bible. These men, humble and often overlooked by society, were chosen by God to receive the first announcement of the Savior's birth. Their story begins in the quiet fields outside Bethlehem, where they kept watch over their flocks by night. The darkness of the evening enveloped them, and their task was simple yet demanding—protect the sheep from predators and ensure their safety. Little did they know that this ordinary night would be transformed into a moment of divine revelation. As they tended their flocks, an angel of the Lord suddenly appeared, and the glory of the Lord shone round about them, piercing the darkness with a brilliance that left them trembling with fear (Luke 2:9). The shepherds, unaccustomed to such a heavenly encounter, were filled with awe, their hearts racing as they tried to comprehend what was happening.

The angel's first words, "Fear not," must have calmed their trembling hearts, offering reassurance in the midst of their astonishment. The angel continued with a message that would change their lives forever: "For, behold, I bring you good tidings of great joy, which shall be to all people. For unto you is born this day in the city of David a Saviour, which is Christ the Lord" (Luke 2:10-11). These words, filled with hope and promise, carried a message of unparalleled significance—the Messiah, long-awaited by generations, had been born. The angel then gave them a sign to confirm this miraculous news: "Ye shall find the babe wrapped in swaddling clothes, lying in a manger" (Luke 2:12). This humble sign was a reflection of God's heart, revealing that the Savior had come not in grandeur but in humility, accessible to all, including the lowliest of society.

As the angel finished speaking, the heavens erupted with praise, and a multitude of the heavenly host appeared, lifting their voices in a song of glory and peace: "Glory to God in the highest, and on earth peace, good will toward men" (Luke 2:14). The shepherds, surrounded by the radiant light and the resounding harmony of angelic worship, must have been overwhelmed by the magnitude of what they were witnessing. The heavens were declaring the glory of God, and they were chosen to be the first recipients of this divine announcement. Their faith began to take root in this moment, as they listened to the angels' proclamation and felt the weight of its truth settle in their hearts.

When the angels departed and the sky returned to its quiet darkness, the shepherds were left with a choice. They could have doubted what they had seen and heard, dismissing it as an impossible dream, or they could believe and act on the message they had received. Their response was one of immediate faith and obedience. They said to one another, "Let us now go even unto Bethlehem, and see this thing which is come to pass, which the Lord hath made known unto us" (Luke 2:15). With urgency and determination, they left their flocks behind and set out for Bethlehem, their hearts burning with the desire to see the Savior for themselves. Their faith was not passive; it was active and alive, driving them to seek the truth and to witness the fulfillment of God's promise.

As they arrived in Bethlehem, the shepherds found everything just as the angel had said. They came to the stable and saw Mary, Joseph, and the baby lying in a manger. This scene, so simple yet so profound, must have filled them with awe and wonder. The child before them was the Messiah, the one who had been promised for generations, the Savior who would bring redemption and peace to a broken world. The shepherds knelt in worship, their hearts overflowing with gratitude and joy. They had come from the fields to the Savior, and their faith had led them to the greatest moment of their lives—the moment when they beheld the Word made flesh, dwelling among them (John 1:14).

The shepherds did not keep this experience to themselves. Filled with the joy of what they had seen and heard, they became the first evangelists, spreading the good news of Jesus' birth to all who would listen. "And when they had seen it, they made known abroad the saying which was told them concerning this child" (Luke 2:17). Their testimony was simple yet powerful, a declaration of the truth that the Savior had come. The people who heard their words marveled at the message, and the shepherds' faith and joy became a beacon of hope for others. Their willingness to share the good news reminds us of the call to bear witness to the work of God in our own lives, to proclaim His glory and His grace to a world in need.

As the shepherds returned to their fields, their lives were forever changed. They glorified and praised God for all they had heard and seen, rejoicing in the truth of His faithfulness and the wonder of His plan (Luke 2:20). Their faith, which had begun with fear and awe in the presence of the angel, grew into a deep and abiding trust in the promises of God. The journey from the fields to the Savior was not just a physical journey but a spiritual one, a movement from doubt to belief, from fear to joy, and from ordinary shepherds to witnesses of the divine.

The shepherds' faith challenges us to respond to God's call with the same immediacy and trust. Their story reminds us that God often reveals His glory to the humble and the lowly, those who are willing to listen and to act on His word. It is a testament to the truth that faith is not just about hearing but about doing, about stepping out in trust and following the path that God has set before us. The shepherds' journey to the Savior is a picture of what it means to seek God with all our hearts, to leave behind the familiar and the comfortable, and to pursue Him with a faith that is bold and unwavering.

Their story also reminds us that God's message of salvation is for all people. The angels proclaimed good tidings of great joy for everyone, and the shepherds, as the first recipients of this message, became symbols of God's inclusive love. Their humble status did not exclude them from the greatest announcement in history; instead, it highlighted the truth that God's grace is available to all, regardless of status or position. The shepherds' faith calls us to embrace this truth and to share the good news with others, to become messengers of hope and witnesses to the light of Christ in a world often overshadowed by darkness.

As we reflect on the shepherds' journey from the fields to the Savior, we are reminded of the importance of faith that moves us to action. Their story is a call to trust in God's promises, to respond to His call with boldness and obedience, and to glorify Him in all that we do. It is a testament to the transformative power of encountering the Savior, a reminder that once we have seen Him, we can never be the same. Let us, like the shepherds, seek the Savior with all our hearts, worship Him with joy and gratitude, and proclaim His glory to the world, for He is the fulfillment of God's promises, the Light of the world, and the hope of all humanity.

Day 27 - The Gold

The gift of gold, presented to the Christ child by the wise men, was more than just a valuable treasure; it was a profound acknowledgment of His identity as the King of Kings, the sovereign ruler whose reign would endure forever. Gold, a precious and enduring metal, has long been associated with royalty, wealth, and honor, a fitting tribute to the One who was born to reign over all nations and whose kingdom would have no end. The wise men, learned scholars from the East who studied the stars and sought the truth, recognized in the star they followed the sign of a king's birth. They traveled a great distance, driven by faith and curiosity, their hearts filled with anticipation and reverence. When they arrived in Bethlehem and found the child with His mother, Mary, they fell down and worshiped Him, presenting their gifts of gold, frankincense, and myrrh as offerings of love, devotion, and recognition of His divine and royal nature (Matthew 2:11). The gold they gave symbolized the majesty and authority of the Christ child, a treasure fit for the King of Kings, the Lord of Lords, and the Savior of the world.

The significance of gold in this moment reaches beyond its material value. It was a declaration of Jesus' kingship, a recognition that He was not merely a child born in humble circumstances but the fulfillment of centuries of prophecy and the divine plan of salvation. The prophets had foretold of a ruler who would come from the house of David, a King whose reign would bring peace, justice, and righteousness to the earth. Isaiah proclaimed, "For unto us a child is born, unto us a son is given: and the government shall be upon His shoulder: and His name shall be called Wonderful, Counsellor, The mighty God, The everlasting Father, The Prince of Peace" (Isaiah 9:6). The gift of gold was a testament to the truth of these prophecies, an acknowledgment that this child was indeed the promised King, sent by God to reign in power and glory.

As the wise men knelt before Jesus, offering their gold, they demonstrated their understanding of His divine authority and their submission to His kingship. Their journey, long and arduous, reflected their determination to honor the King they believed had been born. They followed the star with faith, seeking the One who would bring hope and salvation to the world. Their act of presenting gold was not merely a gesture of respect but an act of worship, a declaration that this child was worthy of the highest honor and the greatest gifts. The gold they offered symbolized their recognition of Jesus' eternal reign, a reign not limited by earthly boundaries or human power but established by the sovereignty of God.

The gift of gold also foreshadowed the nature of Jesus' kingship, a kingship unlike any the world had known. While earthly kings rule with might and seek power, Jesus came to reign through love, humility, and sacrifice. His kingdom was not of this world (John 18:36), and His throne was not adorned with gold but with the hearts of those who believed in Him. The gold given by the wise men pointed to the glory and majesty of His eternal kingdom, a kingdom that would be built not on wealth or conquest but on grace, mercy, and truth. This child, born in a stable and laid in a manger, was the King who would transform the world, the Savior who would bring light to the darkness and life to the weary.

The significance of the gold also lies in its enduring value, a symbol of the eternal nature of Christ's reign. Gold does not tarnish or decay; it remains precious and pure, reflecting the unchanging character of the King it was given to honor. Jesus, the King of Kings, is the same yesterday, today, and forever (Hebrews 13:8), His authority and glory unshaken by time or circumstance. The gold presented to Him by the wise men was a fitting tribute to His eternal kingship, a recognition that His reign would surpass all earthly kingdoms and endure forever. It was a declaration that Jesus is the true King, the One who holds all power and authority in His hands, the One to whom every knee shall bow and every tongue confess (Philippians 2:10-11).

The gift of gold also serves as a reminder of the cost of worship and the value of giving our best to the King. The wise men brought their finest treasures, offering them with hearts full of faith and adoration. Their act of giving challenges us to consider what we bring to the feet of Jesus. Do we offer Him the best of our time, talents, and resources, or do we hold back, giving Him only what is convenient? The gold reminds us that true worship involves sacrifice, a willingness to lay down what we value most as an expression of our love and devotion. It calls us to honor Jesus as the King of our lives, to surrender our hearts to His rule, and to live in a way that reflects His glory and His grace.

The story of the wise men and their gift of gold also speaks to the universal nature of Jesus' kingship. The wise men were Gentiles, travelers from a distant land, yet they recognized the significance of His birth and came to worship Him. Their journey and their offering were a fulfillment of the prophecy that all nations would come to the light of the Messiah, bringing gifts and proclaiming His praise (Isaiah 60:3, 6). The gold they gave was a symbol of the homage owed to the King by all people, a declaration that Jesus is not just the King of the Jews but the King of all nations, the Savior of the world. Their gift reminds us that Jesus' reign is for everyone, and His kingdom is open to all who believe in Him.

As we reflect on the gift of gold, we are reminded of the incredible gift that Jesus Himself is to us. He is the King who left the glory of heaven to walk among us, the Savior who gave His life to redeem us, and the Lord who reigns with justice and love. The gold given to Him by the wise men was a fitting tribute to His majesty, but it pales in comparison to the gift He offers us—the gift of salvation, the promise of eternal life, and the assurance of His unending love. Let us, like the wise men, offer our best to Him, worship Him with all our hearts, and proclaim His glory to the world.

The gold, a gift for the King of Kings, carries a message of honor, worship, and eternal significance. It reminds us of who Jesus is—the sovereign ruler, the promised Messiah, and the Savior of all. It challenges us to live as citizens of His kingdom, to bow before Him in humility and reverence, and to declare His greatness in all that we do. Let us, like the wise men, bring our finest gifts to the feet of Jesus, honoring Him as the King of Kings and the Lord of Lords, the One who is worthy of all glory, praise, and adoration forever.

Day 28 - The Frankincense

The gift of frankincense, presented to the Christ child by the wise men, was a deeply symbolic offering that spoke of worship, divinity, and the sacred nature of Jesus' mission. Frankincense, a fragrant resin harvested from the bark of specific trees, was highly prized in the ancient world for its use in religious ceremonies and worship. When burned, its sweet-smelling smoke ascended to the heavens, symbolizing prayers rising to God. By presenting this gift to Jesus, the wise men acknowledged His divinity, His role as the mediator between God and man, and the holiness of His presence. This was no ordinary child; this was the Son of God, the one anointed to bring salvation to the world, and frankincense was a fitting tribute to His divine nature. The wise men, after following the star to Bethlehem, bowed before the child and opened their treasures, offering frankincense as an act of worship, an acknowledgment that the one before them was worthy of the highest praise and adoration (Matthew 2:11).

The significance of frankincense lies in its association with worship and the sacred. Throughout the Old Testament, frankincense was used in the worship of God, particularly in the tabernacle and temple. The Lord commanded its inclusion in the holy incense, a mixture that was burned before the Ark of the Covenant as an offering to Him (Exodus 30:34-36). Its fragrant aroma filled the air, signifying the prayers of the people and the presence of God's holiness. By offering frankincense to Jesus, the wise men were declaring that He was more than a king; He was divine, the very presence of God in human form. They recognized that this child, born in the humblest of settings, was Immanuel—God with us (Isaiah 7:14; Matthew 1:23). Their gift of frankincense was not only an act of worship but a prophetic acknowledgment of Jesus' role as the ultimate High Priest who would intercede for humanity.

Frankincense also symbolized Jesus' perfect righteousness and His role as the mediator between a holy God and sinful humanity. The sweet-smelling incense that rose to the heavens was a reminder of the purity and holiness required to approach God, a purity that could only be fulfilled in Christ. The wise men, in their act of giving, were pointing to the truth that Jesus would become the bridge between heaven and earth, the one who would reconcile humanity to God. As the writer of Hebrews later explained, "For we have not an high priest which cannot be touched with the feeling of our infirmities; but was in all points tempted like as we are, yet without sin" (Hebrews 4:15). Jesus' sinless life and His willingness to offer Himself as the ultimate sacrifice made Him the fulfillment of what the incense symbolized—the pleasing aroma of perfect obedience and surrender to God's will.

The gift of frankincense also foreshadowed Jesus' role in bringing humanity into the presence of God. In the temple, only the high priest could enter the Holy of Holies, and even then, only once a year, carrying the blood of a sacrifice and the fragrant incense to atone for the sins of the people. Jesus, as the true High Priest, would offer not the blood of animals but His own blood, once for all, to cleanse humanity from sin and open the way to God (Hebrews 9:11-12). The wise men's gift of frankincense, given to the child in Bethlehem, pointed to this ultimate act of worship and sacrifice, a reminder that Jesus came not only to reign as King but to serve as the perfect mediator who would bring reconciliation between God and man.

The act of presenting frankincense was also an act of personal devotion and surrender. The wise men traveled a great distance, enduring hardships and uncertainty, driven by their faith and the hope of finding the one foretold by prophecy. When they saw the child, they fell to their knees and worshiped, opening their treasures and offering the best they had. Their gift of frankincense reflected their recognition of Jesus' divinity and their willingness to honor Him with the finest they could give. Their actions challenge us to examine our own worship—do we approach Jesus with the same reverence and awe? Do we bring Him the best of our hearts, our time, and our devotion, or do we hold back, offering Him only what is convenient? The wise men's gift of frankincense reminds us that true worship requires sacrifice, a willingness to give of ourselves fully and completely in recognition of who Jesus is.

The fragrant aroma of frankincense also symbolizes the prayers and worship of the faithful, rising to God as a sweet-smelling offering. In the book of Revelation, the prayers of the saints are described as incense before the throne of God: "And another angel came and stood at the altar, having a golden censer; and there was given unto him much incense, that he should offer it with the prayers of all saints upon the golden altar which was before the throne. And the smoke of the incense, which came with the prayers of the saints, ascended up before God out of the angel's hand" (Revelation 8:3-4). The gift of frankincense, given to Jesus, reminds us of the importance of prayer and worship in our own lives. Just as the wise men bowed before the Savior and offered their gift, we are called to approach Him with hearts of gratitude and adoration, lifting our prayers and praises to Him as a sweet-smelling sacrifice.

The gift of frankincense also speaks to the universal nature of Jesus' mission. The wise men, Gentiles from a distant land, recognized the significance of His birth and came to worship Him. Their offering of frankincense was a declaration that Jesus was not just the Savior of Israel but the Savior of the world, the one who would bring salvation to all who believe in Him. Their act of worship foreshadowed the inclusion of all nations in God's redemptive plan, a fulfillment of the prophecy that "the Gentiles shall come to thy light, and kings to the brightness of thy rising" (Isaiah 60:3). The gift of frankincense reminds us that Jesus' love and salvation are for everyone, and it calls us to join in the worship of the one who came to bring light and life to all people.

As we reflect on the gift of frankincense, we are reminded of the incredible gift that Jesus Himself is to us. He is the one who brings us into the presence of God, the one who intercedes for us, and the one who is worthy of all worship and praise. The wise men's offering of frankincense challenges us to honor Jesus as our High Priest, to recognize His holiness, and to surrender our lives to Him in worship. It is a call to bring the best of what we have and who we are, to lay it at His feet, and to lift our hearts in adoration of the one who is worthy of all glory and honor.

The frankincense, a gift of worship, carries a message of devotion, divinity, and the sacredness of Jesus' mission. It reminds us of who He is—the sinless Son of God, the perfect High Priest, and the one who brings us into the presence of the Father. Let us, like the wise men, bow before Him in worship, offering our hearts as a fragrant offering, and proclaiming His glory to the world. For Jesus is worthy of all our praise, the one who reigns in righteousness, and the one who has made a way for us to draw near to God. Let us lift our voices, our prayers, and our lives as a sweet-smelling sacrifice to the King of Kings and Lord of Lords, honoring Him with the devotion He so richly deserves.

Day 29 - The Myrrh

The gift of myrrh, brought by the wise men to the Christ child, was a profound and bittersweet offering, rich in meaning and heavy with foreshadowing. Myrrh, a fragrant resin derived from the bark of certain trees, was highly valued in the ancient world for its use in perfumes, anointing oils, and burial preparations. Its deep, earthy aroma carried with it a sense of solemnity and sacredness, making it a fitting gift for the Savior of the world. When the wise men presented this gift to Jesus, alongside gold and frankincense, they were not merely offering a valuable treasure; they were proclaiming the purpose of His life and the depth of His mission. While gold symbolized His kingship and frankincense His divinity, myrrh spoke of His suffering, His humanity, and His ultimate act of redemption. It was a gift that pointed to the cross, to the sacrifice He would make, and to the hope and salvation He would bring to a world lost in sin.

The myrrh, given to a child lying in a manger, was a somber reminder that Jesus was born to die. From the moment of His miraculous conception, His life was marked by a divine purpose—to be the Lamb of God who would take away the sin of the world (John 1:29). The prophets had long foretold the coming of a Savior who would bear the iniquities of humanity, who would be wounded for our transgressions and bruised for our iniquities (Isaiah 53:5). Myrrh, often used in the embalming of the dead, symbolized the suffering and death that awaited Jesus, the sacrifice He would willingly make for the redemption of mankind. It was a gift that carried with it the weight of His mission, a declaration that the child before them was the one who would fulfill God's plan of salvation.

As the wise men knelt before Jesus, offering their gifts, they may not have fully understood the significance of the myrrh they presented, but their act of giving was a reflection of God's divine plan. Myrrh, with its connection to anointing and burial, pointed to Jesus as the Anointed One, the Messiah who would be consecrated for the greatest act of love and obedience. In the Old Testament, anointing with oil was a sign of God's blessing and calling, used to set apart priests, prophets, and kings for their divine purpose. Jesus, the Christ (a title meaning "the Anointed One"), was all three—prophet, priest, and king.

The myrrh given to Him as a child foreshadowed the anointing of His body after His crucifixion, when faithful followers would come to the tomb with spices to honor Him in death (Mark 16:1).

The gift of myrrh also spoke of Jesus' humanity, His willingness to take on flesh and dwell among us (John 1:14). Though He was fully God, He became fully human, experiencing the pain, sorrow, and suffering of this broken world. Myrrh, often used to soothe pain and provide relief, symbolized the suffering He would endure on behalf of humanity. From the agony of Gethsemane to the excruciating pain of the cross, Jesus bore the weight of the world's sin, enduring the punishment that we deserved. "Surely He hath borne our griefs, and carried our sorrows" (Isaiah 53:4). The myrrh was a reminder that the child in the manger was also the man of sorrows, acquainted with grief, who would walk the path of suffering to bring us peace and healing.

At the same time, the myrrh pointed to the hope and victory found in Jesus' sacrifice. While it symbolized death, it also carried the promise of resurrection and redemption. Jesus' death on the cross was not the end but the culmination of God's plan to reconcile humanity to Himself. Through His death, He conquered sin, and through His resurrection, He defeated death, offering eternal life to all who believe in Him. The myrrh, with its association with burial, reminded us that Jesus' body would not see corruption (Psalm 16:10) and that He would rise again, triumphant over the grave. The myrrh, a gift for redemption, was a testament to the power of God's love and the depth of His grace, a symbol of the hope that springs eternal from the cross and the empty tomb.

The wise men's offering of myrrh also challenges us to reflect on the cost of our redemption. The salvation we receive so freely came at the highest price—the life of the Son of God. The myrrh reminds us of the suffering Jesus endured, the nails driven into His hands and feet, the crown of thorns pressed into His brow, and the weight of our sin that He bore on the cross. "But God commendeth His love toward us, in that, while we were yet sinners, Christ died for us" (Romans 5:8). The gift of myrrh calls us to live in gratitude for this incredible sacrifice, to honor Jesus with lives that reflect His love and to share the message of His redemption with a world in need.

The story of the myrrh also invites us to consider our own response to Jesus. The wise men brought their finest treasures, offering them with hearts full of faith and devotion. Myrrh, though it symbolized suffering, was given in hope and reverence, a recognition of the profound gift that Jesus Himself is to us. What do we bring to the Savior? Do we offer Him our best, our whole hearts, and our lives surrendered to His will? The myrrh reminds us that worship involves sacrifice, a willingness to give of ourselves fully and completely in recognition of who Jesus is and what He has done for us.

As we reflect on the myrrh, we are reminded of the depth of God's love for us. He sent His Son into the world not to condemn it but to save it (John 3:17), and the myrrh was a symbol of the cost of that salvation. It speaks of the pain Jesus endured, the death He died, and the victory He achieved. It reminds us that our redemption was not an afterthought, but a plan set in motion from the foundation of the world, a plan fulfilled in the life, death, and resurrection of Jesus Christ.

The myrrh, a gift for redemption, is a symbol of Jesus' mission and a call to worship the One who gave everything for us. It challenges us to live in the light of His sacrifice, to honor Him with our lives, and to proclaim His love to the world. Let us, like the wise men, bring our gifts to the Savior, laying them at His feet and acknowledging Him as the Redeemer, the King, and the Lord of all. The myrrh reminds us of the incredible cost of our salvation and the immeasurable worth of the one who paid it, calling us to worship Him with hearts full of gratitude, love, and devotion.

Day 30 - The Humble King

The birth of Jesus Christ, the humble King born in a lowly place, is a story that defies human expectations and reveals the heart of God's plan for humanity—a plan rooted in love, humility, and redemption. When the Creator of the universe chose to enter His creation, He did not come in grandeur or splendor but in the most unexpected and humble of circumstances. Jesus, the King of Kings and Lord of Lords, was not born in a palace surrounded by wealth and power, but in a stable, a place meant for animals, where the air was filled with the earthy smells of hay and livestock. His first bed was not a cradle crafted by skilled hands but a manger, a feeding trough for animals, rough and unpolished. This was the setting for the arrival of the Savior, the one who would change the course of history and bring hope to a broken world. The lowliness of His birth was no accident; it was a deliberate choice, a declaration of the kind of King He came to be—not one who sought earthly power but one who came to serve and to save, to lift the lowly and humble the proud, and to draw near to those often overlooked and forgotten.

Mary and Joseph, chosen by God to be the earthly parents of Jesus, were themselves humble and unassuming. Mary, a young woman from Nazareth, and Joseph, a carpenter, were not people of wealth or influence, yet they were chosen for this extraordinary purpose because of their faith and obedience. When Mary learned from the angel Gabriel that she would conceive and bear the Son of God, her response was one of humility and trust: "Behold the handmaid of the Lord; be it unto me according to thy word" (Luke 1:38). Joseph, too, displayed quiet strength and faith when he obeyed the angel's command to take Mary as his wife, despite the unusual and miraculous circumstances of her pregnancy (Matthew 1:24). Together, they embarked on the journey to Bethlehem, following the decree of Caesar Augustus that all should be taxed, a journey that brought them to the place where prophecy would be fulfilled.

The journey to Bethlehem was arduous and uncomfortable, especially for Mary, who was heavy with child. The road was long, and the terrain was rough, but Mary and Joseph pressed on, trusting that God was leading them. When they arrived in Bethlehem, they found the town crowded with travelers, and there was no room for them in the inn. This rejection could have been disheartening, but God had prepared a place for His Son to be born, a stable where the King of Glory would make His entrance into the world. In that humble setting, under the watchful eyes of Joseph and surrounded by the quiet presence of animals, Mary brought forth her firstborn son. She wrapped Him in swaddling clothes and laid Him in a manger, a moment of profound simplicity that carried the weight of eternity (Luke 2:7).

The lowliness of Jesus' birth was a reflection of His mission. He came not to be served but to serve and to give His life as a ransom for many (Matthew 20:28). His birth in a stable, far from the trappings of wealth and power, was a testament to His identification with the humble and the poor. Throughout His ministry, Jesus would continue to show compassion to the marginalized, the outcasts, and the sinners, offering them hope and redemption. His humble beginnings were a sign that His kingdom was not of this world (John 18:36), a kingdom where the last would be first, and the greatest would be the servant of all. The stable and the manger were not symbols of weakness but of God's power to work through the lowly and the ordinary to accomplish His extraordinary purposes.

The announcement of Jesus' birth was also a reflection of His humility. The first to hear the good news were not kings or rulers but shepherds, men of lowly status who kept watch over their flocks by night. An angel of the Lord appeared to them, and the glory of the Lord shone around them, bringing them the message that would change their lives: "Fear not: for, behold, I bring you good tidings of great joy, which shall be to all people. For unto you is born this day in the city of David a Saviour, which is Christ the Lord" (Luke 2:10-11). The shepherds, though unassuming and often overlooked, were invited to witness the miracle of the Savior's birth. They hurried to Bethlehem, where they found Mary, Joseph, and the baby lying in a manger, just as the angel had said. Their response was one of worship and proclamation, as they glorified and praised God for all they had seen and heard (Luke 2:20).

The humility of Jesus' birth also pointed to the sacrifice He would make for the redemption of humanity. From the stable in Bethlehem to the cross at Calvary, Jesus' life was marked by humility and selflessness. The manger, rough and simple, foreshadowed the wood of the cross, where He would lay down His life for the sins of the world. The King who was born in a stable would one day wear a crown of thorns, bearing the punishment we deserved so that we might be reconciled to God. "Let this mind be in you, which was also in Christ Jesus: Who, being in the form of God, thought it not robbery to be equal with God: But made Himself of no reputation, and took upon Him the form of a servant, and was made in the likeness of men" (Philippians 2:5-7). Jesus' humble birth was a reflection of His willingness to step down from the glory of heaven and enter into the brokenness of our world to bring healing, hope, and salvation.

The humility of Jesus' birth is also a reminder of the kind of hearts God values. The stable and the manger teach us that God is not impressed by wealth, status, or power; He looks at the heart. Just as He chose Mary and Joseph for their faith and obedience, He calls us to approach Him with humility and surrender. The lowliness of the King born in Bethlehem invites us to lay down our pride, to recognize our need for a Savior, and to come to Him with childlike faith. "Blessed are the poor in spirit: for theirs is the kingdom of heaven" (Matthew 5:3). The story of Jesus' birth challenges us to see that greatness in God's kingdom is found not in exalting ourselves but in humbling ourselves before Him.

As we reflect on the birth of the humble King, we are reminded of the depth of God's love for us. He chose to enter the world in the most vulnerable and unassuming way, to walk among us, and to experience the joys and sorrows of human life. His humility was a demonstration of His willingness to meet us where we are, to enter into our brokenness, and to bring us into His light. The stable in Bethlehem, though small and insignificant in the eyes of the world, became the birthplace of the greatest gift ever given—the gift of Jesus Christ, our Savior and King.

The humility of Jesus' birth is a call to worship and gratitude. It reminds us that God's ways are not our ways, and His thoughts are not our thoughts (Isaiah 55:8-9). He chose the lowly to accomplish His purposes, demonstrating that His power is made perfect in weakness (2 Corinthians 12:9). The King born in a lowly place invites us to bow before Him, to give Him our hearts, and to follow Him with lives marked by humility, love, and service. Let us, like the shepherds, come to the manger with awe and wonder, glorifying and praising God for the gift of His Son, the humble King who came to bring us peace, joy, and salvation. For in the lowliness of His birth, we see the greatness of His love, the depth of His grace, and the beauty of His kingdom, a kingdom that will reign forever and ever.

Day 31 – Emmanuel

Emmanuel, meaning "God with us," is one of the most profound and comforting truths ever revealed to humanity, a declaration of God's unending love and His desire to dwell among His creation. This name, first spoken through the prophet Isaiah, carries a promise that stretches across the ages: "Behold, a virgin shall conceive, and bear a son, and shall call His name Immanuel" (Isaiah 7:14). When Jesus was born in Bethlehem, this prophecy was fulfilled, and the eternal Word of God took on flesh, walking among us as a living testament to God's faithfulness and grace. The name Emmanuel encapsulates the very essence of who Jesus is and why He came, for in Him, the fullness of God dwells, and through Him, the barrier between humanity and the divine is torn down. The birth of Emmanuel was not merely the arrival of a great teacher or prophet; it was the physical manifestation of God's presence with His people, a tangible expression of His desire to redeem and restore a broken world.

The reality of Emmanuel, God with us, begins with the miraculous conception of Jesus. Mary, a young virgin, was chosen to bear the Son of God, a child conceived by the Holy Ghost. When the angel Gabriel appeared to her, he declared, "The Holy Ghost shall come upon thee, and the power of the Highest shall overshadow thee: therefore also that holy thing which shall be born of thee shall be called the Son of God" (Luke 1:35). This miracle was the moment when the infinite God chose to enter the finite, when the Creator stepped into His creation, not as a distant and untouchable deity but as a humble and approachable Savior. The name Emmanuel speaks to the mystery of the incarnation, the truth that Jesus was fully God and fully man, a bridge between heaven and earth. His birth was the culmination of God's promise to be with His people, not in fleeting moments or temporary glimpses, but in the fullness of His glory and grace.

The significance of Emmanuel lies in the truth that God came to dwell among us in our brokenness. Jesus was born in the humblest of settings, not in a palace or a place of power, but in a stable, wrapped in swaddling clothes and laid in a manger. His lowly birth was a reflection of His mission to seek and save the lost, to draw near to the humble, the hurting, and the outcast. Emmanuel,

God with us, means that we are not alone in our struggles, our sorrows, or our fears. Jesus came to walk where we walk, to feel what we feel, and to carry the burdens that weigh us down. "For we have not an high priest which cannot be touched with the feeling of our infirmities; but was in all points tempted like as we are, yet without sin" (Hebrews 4:15). In Emmanuel, we see a God who does not stand far off but comes close, entering into our lives with compassion, understanding, and an unshakable love.

Throughout His earthly ministry, Jesus demonstrated what it meant to be Emmanuel. He healed the sick, gave sight to the blind, and brought the dead back to life, revealing the power and presence of God at work in the world. He spoke words of hope and truth to the weary and the brokenhearted, extending forgiveness to sinners and offering peace to those burdened by guilt and shame. Emmanuel means that God is not a distant observer but an active participant in the lives of His people, bringing healing, restoration, and redemption. His presence was a light in the darkness, a beacon of hope for all who would turn to Him. Jesus declared, "I am the light of the world: he that followeth me shall not walk in darkness, but shall have the light of life" (John 8:12). In Emmanuel, we see the fulfillment of this promise, a God who illuminates our path and leads us into the fullness of His love.

The ultimate expression of Emmanuel is found in the cross. Jesus, the sinless Son of God, took upon Himself the weight of humanity's sin, bearing the punishment we deserved so that we could be reconciled to God. The name Emmanuel reminds us that God did not leave us in our sin but entered into it, taking it upon Himself to redeem us. "But God commendeth His love toward us, in that, while we were yet sinners, Christ died for us" (Romans 5:8). On the cross, Emmanuel, God with us, became God for us, offering Himself as the perfect sacrifice to bridge the gap between a holy God and sinful humanity. His death and resurrection are the ultimate proof of God's love and His commitment to be with His people forever.

The promise of Emmanuel did not end with Jesus' ascension into heaven. Before He returned to the Father, Jesus assured His disciples, "Lo, I am with you alway, even unto the end of the world" (Matthew 28:20). Through the gift of the Holy Spirit, the presence of Emmanuel continues to dwell with and within believers, guiding, comforting, and empowering us to live lives that glorify God. The name Emmanuel is a reminder that God's presence is not confined to a single moment in history but is an eternal reality for those who trust in Him. In every season, every trial, and every joy, Emmanuel remains with us, a constant source of hope and strength.

The message of Emmanuel, God with us, is one of unparalleled hope. It reminds us that we are never alone, no matter how dark or difficult our circumstances may be. It assures us that God is present in our pain, our doubts, and our fears, offering us His peace and His power. "The Lord is nigh unto them that are of a broken heart; and saveth such as be of a contrite spirit" (Psalm 34:18). Emmanuel speaks to the depth of God's love, a love that moved Him to step into our world, to bear our burdens, and to make a way for us to be with Him forever. It is a name that brings comfort to the weary, strength to the weak, and joy to the brokenhearted.

As we reflect on the name Emmanuel, we are called to live in the light of His presence. It is a call to trust in His promises, to rest in His love, and to walk with Him in faith and obedience. Emmanuel reminds us that God is not far away but near, closer than our very breath, and that His desire is to dwell with us and to draw us into a deeper relationship with Him. It is a call to worship, to bow before the One who left the glory of heaven to be with us, to redeem us, and to make us His own. Emmanuel is the assurance that no matter where we are or what we face, God is with us, guiding us, sustaining us, and leading us home.

The name Emmanuel, God with us, is the heartbeat of the gospel, the message of a God who loves us so deeply that He came to dwell among us, to walk with us, and to save us. It is a name that changes everything, a reminder that we are never alone and that we are deeply loved. Let us, with hearts full of gratitude and awe, embrace the truth of Emmanuel, living in the joy and peace of His presence, and proclaiming the wonder of His love to a world in need of hope. Emmanuel, God with us, is the greatest gift we could ever receive, the fulfillment of God's promise to be near, and the assurance of His unending love and faithfulness.

Conclusion

AS WE CLOSE THIS JOURNEY through The Characters of Christmas, let us carry with us the profound lessons these people and places teach us about faith, obedience, humility, and the unfathomable love of God. The Christmas story is not just a historical event; it is a living invitation to experience the miracle of God's presence in our lives today. Mary's unwavering faith reminds us to trust God even when His plans stretch beyond our understanding, for His promises are always true, and His timing is perfect. Joseph's quiet obedience inspires us to follow God's direction with courage, even when the path is uncertain or difficult. The shepherds' joy-filled response to the angelic announcement calls us to step out of our routines and seek Him with a heart eager to worship. The wise men's relentless pursuit of the Savior urges us to keep seeking Jesus no matter the distance, knowing that the journey is worth every sacrifice. These characters, though imperfect and human like us, were used by God to bring His eternal plan to life, proving that He works through ordinary people who are willing to say yes to His call.

The places of Christmas also hold a mirror to our spiritual walk. Bethlehem, the small town chosen for the birth of the King, reminds us that God often works in the humble and overlooked spaces of our lives to bring about His glory. The stable and the manger, symbols of simplicity and humility, call us to lay down our pride and welcome Christ into the unpolished corners of our hearts. The fields where shepherds watched their flocks teach us that even in the mundane tasks of everyday life, God can break through with a message of hope and purpose. The journey of the wise men reveals that God's light will guide us through any darkness if we are willing to follow Him. Even Herod's fear and rejection serve as a sobering reminder that we must guard our hearts from allowing pride and self-interest to blind us to the gift of Jesus.

For the Christian today, the story of Christmas is a blueprint for walking faithfully with the Lord. It calls us to trust God with our uncertainties, to rejoice in His presence, and to share the good news of His love with a world in desperate need of hope. Mary's song of praise, "My soul doth magnify the Lord, and my spirit hath rejoiced in God my Saviour" (Luke 1:46-47), is an anthem we too can sing as we reflect on God's goodness and faithfulness in our lives. Joseph's willingness to protect and provide for his family, even at great personal cost, challenges us to live sacrificially and put others before ourselves. The angels' proclamation of "peace on earth, good will toward men" (Luke 2:14) is a reminder to carry God's peace into our relationships and to let His love shine through us in every interaction. The shepherds' urgency to spread the news of Christ's birth compels us to boldly share the gospel, proclaiming the joy and salvation that Jesus brings.

The Christmas story also reminds us that God's plans are often unexpected but always perfect. He chose the humble, the overlooked, and the faithful to play pivotal roles in the greatest story ever told. In the same way, He calls us—ordinary people with flaws and doubts—to be part of His extraordinary work. The characters of Christmas teach us that God doesn't require perfection; He desires a willing heart. Just as He used a young virgin, a carpenter, shepherds, and wise men, He can use us to reflect His glory and further His kingdom. Our walk with the Lord is not about what we bring to the table but about our willingness to surrender to His will, trusting that His power is made perfect in our weakness (2 Corinthians 12:9).

As Christians, we are called to embody the spirit of Christmas every day, to live with the joy, peace, and hope that Christ's birth brings. Emmanuel, "God with us," is not just a name but a reality for those who follow Him. The same God who entered the world as a humble baby walks with us today, guiding, comforting, and empowering us to live for His glory. The characters of Christmas challenge us to reflect on our own lives and ask, "Am I willing to trust God like Mary? To obey Him like Joseph? To rejoice like the shepherds? To seek Him like the wise men?" Their stories remind us that faith is active—it requires us to take steps toward Him, to worship Him fully, and to let His light shine through us in a dark world.

As we reflect on the people and places of Christmas, let us also remember that the story doesn't end in Bethlehem. The baby in the manger grew to be the Savior on the cross, the risen Lord who conquered sin and death to bring us eternal life. The message of Christmas is the message of the gospel: God loves us so much that He sent His Son to dwell among us, to save us, and to restore us to Himself. This truth changes everything. It transforms how we see ourselves, how we treat others, and how we live each day. It gives us a reason to hope, a reason to worship, and a reason to share the love of Christ with everyone we meet.

As we close this book, may the characters of Christmas inspire you to deepen your walk with the Lord. Let their faith encourage you to trust Him more fully, their obedience challenge you to follow Him more boldly, and their joy remind you of the incredible gift of His presence. The story of Christmas is a story of God's love, a love that reached down into the ordinary to bring about the extraordinary. It is a love that invites us to come as we are, to kneel at the manger, and to leave transformed by the Savior who is Emmanuel—God with us. May we carry this story in our hearts, not just during the Christmas season but throughout our lives, as we walk in faith, live in hope, and share the light of Christ with the world.

Don't miss out!

Visit the website below and you can sign up to receive emails whenever Joshua Rhoades publishes a new book. There's no charge and no obligation.

https://books2read.com/r/B-A-AJLBB-ULJLF

BOOKS 2 READ

Connecting independent readers to independent writers.

Did you love *The Characters of Christmas*? Then you should read *Enabled-Living God's Purpose With Power*[1] by Joshua Rhoades!

[2]

The 31-day devotional, "Enabled: Living God's Purpose With Power", is a refreshing and empowering guide for believers seeking to deepen their relationship with God and walk confidently in His purpose. Through a month-long journey, this devotional brings readers face-to-face with the profound truth that God equips, sustains, and strengthens us to fulfill His calling. Each daily message is centered on Scripture, rooted in the timeless wisdom of the King James Version, and inspired by I Timothy 1:12, where Paul says, "And I thank Christ Jesus our Lord, who hath enabled me." This verse forms the heart of this devotional, reminding us that just as God enabled Paul to overcome immense trials, He provides us with the strength to navigate our own challenges, live with courage, and stay faithful to His purpose.

Life often brings uncertainties, doubts, and fears that weigh us down, making us feel inadequate or overwhelmed. Yet, "Enabled" speaks directly to

---

1. https://books2read.com/u/3Lqy20

2. https://books2read.com/u/3Lqy20

those struggles, encouraging readers to trade their weaknesses for God's boundless strength. Each day's entry includes a Scripture reflection, practical insight, and a heartfelt prayer, making it easy to apply God's truths to everyday life. This book is a powerful reminder that we are never meant to walk the Christian journey alone or rely solely on our own abilities. Rather, God's power is ever-present and available, actively working through us to accomplish His will. Through this devotional, you'll discover the peace that comes from knowing God's strength is made perfect in our weakness, allowing us to live with resilience, hope, and purpose.

As you progress through each day's message, you'll be encouraged by how God empowers us to overcome fear, endure difficult circumstances, serve others with love, and live courageously in every situation. By the end of the 31 days, you'll have a renewed understanding of how to rely on God's strength, not your own, and find that even in the toughest moments, His grace is always sufficient, His love never wavers, and His plans for you are steadfast. Each devotion highlights a unique aspect of God's enabling power, such as courage, peace, endurance, wisdom, and faithfulness, helping you see how His presence enriches every corner of life.

Whether you're facing challenges, feeling uncertain, or simply longing to strengthen your faith, "Enabled: Living God's Purpose With Power" is a perfect companion. This devotional guides you to keep your eyes on Christ, trust His timing, and walk with confidence, knowing you are equipped by His Spirit. It's a beautiful resource for anyone, whether new to the faith or well along in their walk with the Lord. With each day's entry, you'll find yourself empowered, encouraged, and equipped to live out God's calling in your life, discovering that His enabling power isn't just for the heroes of Scripture, but for every believer today—including you. This book becomes a personal guide and source of daily inspiration, helping you build a strong foundation in faith and a life transformed by God's presence.

www.ingramcontent.com/pod-product-compliance
Lightning Source LLC
LaVergne TN
LVHW091111150826
845673LV00002B/782